SMALL COURAGE

A Queer Memoir of Finding Love
and Conceiving Family

JANE BYERS

DAGGER EDITIONS 2020

For my wife, Amy, and to our children, Franny and Theo, without whose courage I would not have mustered my own to write this book.

CONTENTS

PREFACE

On one of our favourite cloudy-day family hikes, our daughter, Franny, tells a story. The hike is on a well-worn trail in Kokanee Creek Provincial Park. It winds through a mixed cedar forest culminating in a waterfall. The creek sometimes rages and sometimes achieves a more mellow descent, though never a serene trickle. It certainly never dries up, nor do any creeks originating from glaciers in our inland temperate rain forest of southern British Columbia. Before we became parents, this would have been our mellow recovery hike the day after a nine-hour rugged lung buster in the alpine.

Telling stories on a hike is not uncommon now that we have children; I have had nine years to grow accustomed to the endless chatter that I used to think of as an intrusion to my meditative and soul-cleansing walks in the woods. Our daughter insists on a story so she can distract herself from her own boredom with hiking, though often my wife and I are the ones tasked with telling the stories.

"Mama, will you tell me another story?"

"It's your turn to tell us a story," Amy, my wife, answers. It is quiet for a minute and I wonder if Franny is dreaming up a tale or has forgotten the question.

Franny slows down in front of a fallen cedar, its splintered trunk still upright, and says, "I am a baby animal, a puppy. I was born on that tree stump right there. My mother breastfed me. A few minutes later Theo was born. Then a cougar killed our mother and we were alone on the tree stump but only for two minutes. Then you came along and found us and we became a forever family."

"How did it feel to be alone for two minutes?" I eventually choke out after picking my jaw up off the trail and quelling my instinct to frame the question negatively. *Were you scared?* is my first instinct.

"It was only two minutes so it was okay," Franny says.

"Your birth mom died? Does it feel like she is dead in real life?" I ask.

"Sometimes it feels like she's not really real," Franny answers.

Franny's twin brother, Theo, says, "Mom, look at that bird in the tree, way up there," while continuing to whack dead branches that didn't make it through the long winter.

"What kind of a bird is it, buddy?" I ask, my eyes too full of tears to see the dirty snow still clinging to the northwest aspect of rocks and cedars, the vibrant green of new growth on the fir saplings or the bird.

"I don't know, maybe a chickadee?"

"Maybe," I say, vaguely noncommittal, as I digest what Franny has just told us. I don't think it's a coincidence that she told an origin story after spending a week of family time together over spring break, during which the four of us were tuned in to one another in attachment-parenting bliss.

Franny is creating a story in which she is resilient. Apparently her ten-year-old self can manage resilience for two minutes. If this is true, I have given her something besides increasing her tolerance for hikes, which has been no small feat in itself. She often says she'd rather be at the mall, which is the place she used to stroll and walk as a toddler with her foster family.

My first poetry collection, *Steeling Effects*, was an attempt not only to answer the question of how any of us, and I in particular, ended up resilient, but also to leave a metaphorical road map for my children. Whatever difficult stories the twins will come to learn about their early beginnings and biological family history, they will also know they come from resilience. Let this be their inheritance.

Once, after seeing a colourful Anne Geddes print in Grandma's front entrance—a well-constructed photo of babies, some bemused, some distracted, some focused, seemingly growing in terracotta flowerpots—Theo, who was seven at the time, said, "See, kids grow from flowers." He said this with a glint in his eye, as if he was daring me to go along with that story and to refute the birth-mother/adoption story we had told him all along.

I pointed out the brown-skinned boy in the print and said, "Yes, that's you." His obvious delight told me he could live with this flowerpot origin story even if I always thought the print a little creepy for its juxtaposition of plants and children.

When I was a child, the closest I felt to my mother was in the rare times she would tell me about my birth. At first she didn't tell me all the details of my near death, or of hers, or that they said I would likely be institutionalized because I was without oxygen for too long. Perhaps she didn't tell me this until I was a teenager.

My story evolves too, as I gain perspective, as I raise children, as I benefit from time and softening with age, though I resist evolution for a rigid grip on what I call *facts*. You see, in my family I am a truth teller and for that I have never been forgiven. "Unhappy families are conspiracies of silence. The one who breaks the silence is never forgiven." So writes Jeanette Winterson in *Why Be Happy When You Could Be Normal?* At some point I realized I must forgive myself, but this is the work of a life, forever in progress.

Back on the waterfall trail, I'm even more in awe of my daughter's story, her ability to tell it at ten years old, that she embraces the story and how it evolves. I have given her some notion of how important stories are in our lives and I do feel this is a major accomplishment. I'm not certain I have the same resilience. Not the concrete block kind, but the tensile strength of a spiderweb, many times stronger than concrete—that strength that absorbs new information and is intact, the kind that temporarily inhabits trauma along the journey but moves on to a full life.

We all want to be seen, to have someone who is curious about us. I yearned to be seen, still do, I'm slightly embarrassed to say. In many ways, not being well seen has motivated my parenting. The Irish novelist Anne Enright says that to see others as they really are, without trying to change them, is an act of empathy. I am determined to see my children—who they are, not who I wish them to be.

Perhaps, like Franny, we all tell ourselves stories we can live with. And what we can live with changes.

CONCEIVING FAMILY

We bought our house over the internet: seven pictures and a decent real estate agent who had refused to sell us other junky houses when we were getting desperate to move to the Kootenays from Toronto in 2006. He called us and said, "Girls. This is it. You are going to love it." We faxed an offer from the rundown laundromat around the corner from our flat in Little India, outbidding the others in a hot market, and flew out for the home inspection. We fell in love with the Victorian house at a quiet end of a residential street just a block from the bustling downtown, with a view of Kootenay Lake from the front windows, and fruit trees. The house had a massive deck as large as our one-bedroom apartment in Toronto, and lots of rock walls that terraced our sloped yard. And the inside: high ceilings; charming, if worn, fir floors; a huge kitchen with a working fireplace; two small bedrooms, one of them with a view of the lake; and a main-floor office. Who cared if the ornate brass fireplace in the living room didn't function? This was more charm than we could ever imagine affording in Toronto.

After that first summer of making our house feel like home, being surprised and delighted by cherry and plum blossoms, yellow tulips, purple irises and a magenta peony in our perennial gardens, we decided to take advantage of our easy access to the Rockies and enjoy a mountain adventure. We were ready for couple time after being utterly enchanted all summer: small theatre productions that blew our socks off, early-morning cycling with new friends, even the food co-op where conversations about geopolitics or sprout farming await the willing shopper. As much as a summer in Nelson filled our buckets with beauty, I was eager to finally share a multiday backpacking experience with Amy, one in which we would test our own stamina and access wild places. We pored over our new bible, *Don't Waste Your Time in the Canadian Rockies*, for a five-day premier trip and settled on Mount Assiniboine. I'd signed an employment contract for my new job with the understanding that I could have a week off before Labour Day, knowing that Amy would be starting film school right afterwards. That it also became a "conceiving family" trip was a testament to how unerring and open the rest of our new life together in Nelson felt. I knew the combination of quiet, intense exercise and fresh air was a recipe for a decision that would feel right, down to my core, and hoped it would be the same for Amy. The endurance, interdependence and ups and downs of a backpacking trip seemed an apt metaphor for a couple who can't just *get* pregnant. To have children or not was the question we set out to answer, although we agreed not to talk about it until the trip's end. The backpacking trip transcended the Continental Divide: the point at which water flows either to the Atlantic or to the Pacific, not both.

The first day of backpacking is typically uncomfortable. My body getting accustomed to carrying a heavy pack, my hips settling into their new weight, a weight that is always at its heaviest at the start: five days of food as well as the stove, pots and water filter, tent, sleeping bag and all the clothes, shorts to down jackets, necessary for a thirty-degree range in temperature. Our quiet tramping under a deep-blue September sky through a meadow covered in fresh snow was punctuated, on the first day, by glimpsing a bear a hundred metres off the path, sitting and digging roots.

"Look! It's a grizzly," I said, pointing.

"How do you know it's a grizzly?" Amy asked as she charged forward on the path.

"See the hump on its neck, its dished face? It's digging roots for protein."

"I'm protein," Amy said as she practically broke into a run with eighty pounds on her back.

"It's not interested in you. Besides, they say not to run away from a bear," I yelled at the adrenalin-surged, disappearing figure that was my wife. I too quickened my pace, feeling the jolt I feel only when in the presence of large predators, especially ones that are not separated from us by bars in a zoo. Winded, I finally caught up, a couple of hundred metres later. "Going it alone doesn't help, particularly with grizzlies," I said in between large gulps of water.

I was more accustomed than Amy was to bear sightings on hikes, having spent the summer of 2003 backpacking and hiking in the Rockies, the Purcells and the Selkirks with experienced hikers who instilled that calmness in me. I wasn't complacent, but neither was I particularly concerned.

Our first night, the grizzly close encounter still fresh in my partner's mind, she remained vigilant while I closed my eyes. Outside, fresh bits of snow collected as I tried to cozy up in our zipped-together sleeping bags.

"How can you sleep?" Amy asked with an accusatory tone.

"How can you not?" I countered as my breathing slowed again into near sleep.

She nudged me awake. "What's that noise?"

"A rodent, probably," I said.

"That's bigger than a rodent."

"Yeah, it's probably a bear," I said.

"I'm serious. What if—?"

I cut her off. "Once, when I was camping in the Valhalla wilderness with friends, I heard snuffling and footsteps in the dark. I lay there frozen scared, sure that it was a grizzly. I finally fell back asleep, afraid to wake up my tent mate, telling myself that I would die happy at least. In the morning there were deer tracks and droppings around the tent."

"I get that, but it *sounds* like something much bigger," Amy said.

"Our food is in the food cache; we have nothing they want in the tent. Let's get some sleep." Although still far from settled, Amy let me drape my arm across her merino wool base layer that doubled as pyjamas on hikes.

The rest of the trip was without bear sightings, though a ranger told us that a young male grizzly was lingering near the backcountry lodge and campground. By day two, I could tease Amy about the bear scare. "You were going to go it alone? You were okay with me being mauled by a bear because I was slower than you?" In time I would learn that Amy's anxiety could fuel her head-down barge forward in certain life situations. This wasn't just a one-off.

The icy mammoth of Mount Assiniboine took our breath away as it towered above us at Magog Lake Campground, our base camp for a couple of nights. At 2,378 metres, this was the highest place I'd ever camped, as our iced-over pot of water, poured the night before for coffee, could attest. Still, we were both eager to demonstrate our love by being the first up to get the water boiling.

While my mind wandered on our daily hikes, I pondered *the* question. Sometimes I think being a hermit would suit me, a source of concern with the child question in front of me. It was certainly my father's central battle, how to be with his family and get the quiet alone time he seemed to need. This was a much deeper fear for me than the grizzly in the alpine: how to get the deep contemplative quiet that I seem to need, knowing how at odds this is with parenting. Also, Amy and I had a great life, a great relationship, time to do what we wanted professionally, creatively, recreationally. Why would anyone want to change this? Despite all these rational reasons for maintaining the status quo, I had an answer to *Do I want to start a family with Amy?* but it brought up vulnerable questions: *What if she doesn't? How do we move forward?* On the last day, the descent long but easy for our habituated legs, we reopened the kid conversation as agreed. Despite cleaning my lungs out with alpine air and deep breathing, I could feel my breath catch. "Want to talk about kids?"

"Sure, I'm ready to talk," Amy said.

"How do we want to do this? Who goes first?" I knew my answer but was viscerally aware that a yes could hurt as much as a no if we both didn't come to the same conclusion. Either one of us could wound the other and the relationship with one syllable. I was feeling the vulnerability that perhaps my ex-partner had felt when she brought up having a child and was rebuffed by me. Not that anyone was rebuffing this time around, but what if I wanted this more than Amy did? What if she decided this wasn't the relationship for her or worried that our relationship would not withstand this sea change? I offered to go first, not hampered by my usual inclinations to play it safe, to not offend. I was somewhat surprised by the strength of my own decision and how I so conclusively arrived at it while walking and not even consciously thinking about the question much. "Yes."

"Me too" came the swift reply, followed by hugging. It is hard to hug with backpacks so we doffed them and took a break.

"Wow, okay. What now? I mean, that's awesome." My *yes* seemed as natural as donning my pack and hiking boots by then but neither one of us could rationally explain how we got to that decision. "You aren't worried that our awesome life will be ruined?"

"I think our awesome life will be more awesome. And you aren't worried about having time to write?" she asked.

"Yes, I am, but my answer is still yes. We'll figure it out." The rest of the way down felt like a breeze, as we smiled at each other and allowed our imaginations to wander.

We celebrated by driving to a fancy Calgary hotel. When we pulled up, the valet parked our dust-caked Subaru and we walked into a sparkling lobby, dirty backpacks in hand. The hotel was worth the price just for the luxurious shower that we languished in for what seemed like an hour. There is no better feeling after many days of sweating beneath a large backpack, punctuated only by quick rinses in frigid mountain creeks, than lathering up. And knowing that getting clean was a prelude to lying on a deluxe bed with high-thread-count sheets, while sipping a cold beer, before rustling up dinner at one of the many good restaurants in the neighbourhood. It was there we talked about the next question in our new journey to be parents. I assume most people do not even ask this question. *How?* However many times we consummated our decision, we wouldn't make a baby in the process.

BLUE WONDER

There's a piece of sky in me. That deep blue inhabited me when I was four turning five, looking out of the BOAC 707 plane en route from Manchester to Toronto. We immigrated to Canada from northern England. Had we immigrated just two years before, we would have done so by ship from Liverpool, but the world was changing rapidly with air travel being accessible for commoners. The posh, crisp stewardess stopped at my seat and leaned over, handing me a silver BOAC broach with her glamorous, long, red fingernails. She looked at me and with her perfect teeth formed the words "Hello, would you like to come to the front of the plane and see the cockpit?"

My parents looked at me. "Yes, yes, yes," I said. I followed her impossibly long legs, whose blue pantyhose looked nothing like my grandmother's. The vast blue sky out of the front of the plane and the dark Atlantic below it were bigger than I could ever imagine. I felt wonder.

"What are all those buttons for?" I asked the pilots, all men. They laughed. One of them pointed at the throttle and said, "This makes us go fast." From then on, I wanted to be a stewardess when I grew up. The BOAC wings stayed with me through various childhood moves but I threw them out when I left the nest to set out on my own. It didn't occur to me to want to be the pilot until I brushed up against and challenged my parents' and the world's sexism years later. This was only 1970, the same year *Time* magazine's article, "Who's Come A Long Way, Baby?," was published. It said, we want equal pay for equal work.

We deplaned down a set of steps onto the frozen tarmac into minus-twenty-six-degree temperatures on February 29. It was so cold it took my breath away and made my always rosy cheeks even rosier. My auntie was there to meet us once we got inside the terminal. She had sponsored our family to immigrate and my father being an English-speaking journeyman electrician didn't hurt either, in the eyes of the Canadian officials.

We stayed in the Seahorse Motel along Toronto's Lake Shore Boulevard West until we found an apartment at Yonge and Highway 401. My aunt's small apartment wouldn't house us, though we had many visits with her. Decades later the motel got swallowed up by the urban creep of condo development on the boulevard, before which it sat in squat decline as its vinyl pool chairs faded from neon to pastel and the city modernized around it.

After a short stint in the motel, we moved into our apartment at Yonge and 401 with our two suitcases. With my father's first paycheque from A.G. Simpson, a metal stamping plant, my parents bought me a bed. Eventually they bought a white Formica dining room table with yellow vinyl floral-print chairs. They did this on credit at Bad Boy, a furniture store owned by Mel Lastman, who, twenty-seven years later, would become mayor of Toronto. They got gouged by the interest rate on the loan but had no choice if they wanted furniture. This was pre-credit-card days, or at least when credit cards were not available to my parents. My mom and dad eventually bought themselves a bed on credit but slept on the floor for the first few months. Mel Lastman's tendency to use his power was evident decades later when he would attempt to lean into me, when I was an employee of the City of Toronto. His neighbour was not the successful bidder on the city's lucrative contract for office chairs, a decision I was involved in as part of the city's corporate safety group. As a result, the rest of the committee and I were requested to sit in a meeting with the unsuccessful bidder and subjected to criticism about what was a fair and objective process simply because it wasn't the outcome the mayor's neighbour wanted. To the mayor's credit, ultimately the committee's decision stood.

As a new immigrant, my mother was miserable, having moved what must have felt like an impossible distance from her home and her family. She chose Canada rather than the prospect of having my father rejoin the merchant marine and sail all over the world as a ship's officer, coming home only infrequently for shore leave. Prior to this journey, she had travelled only within England and mostly within Lancashire. Years later, she told me she wanted to die at that time in her life. When she told me this, I knew enough to be glad she didn't say she wanted to kill herself, though in my dark moments I thought less of her for being so passive as to wish for death but do nothing about it. They didn't exactly have immigrant settlement programs, nor did they have Mother Goose programs for young moms and their children where they could sing together and parents could learn how to be present with their children.

Within that first year after immigrating, in a rage, I tried to run through our patio glass door, as if I were the external manifestation of my mother's misery. Nobody remembers the alleged reason for my tantrum in which I smashed the single-paned glass door. Thankfully it was reinforced glass, the kind with a faint grid from embedded wire, so I ended up with only a small cut. I don't remember why but I can only imagine a barely there, depressed mother and the loss of my daily and loving connection with my grandmother contributing. The outdoor time in the green hills being replaced by this sparse apartment near Canada's busiest highway that felt nothing like home couldn't have helped. I can imagine all of these factors led to my expression of defiant anger.

I got teased for my English accent at school but mostly the adults thought it cute. Ah, the privilege of coming from the mother country and of being white, even if a little swarthy. My ancestry remains a question mark despite genetic testing, though if you believe those commercial tests of dubious accuracy, I have some Punjabi ancestry four generations back. I soon lost the English accent though I would always feel like an outsider. In Napanee, where we lived when I was aged nine to sixteen, I liked to remind my friends that I wasn't from there, that I was born in England. I'm sure I had an air of superiority that would make my adult self cringe. Mostly I wanted to differentiate myself from the rest of my classmates, with whom I didn't feel I belonged. I wasn't a farmer; we hadn't lived in the community for generations. I played sports at lunch with all the boys.

My maternal grandmother made me a sky-blue angora wool vest. I both loved and hated this vest. It was itchy and looked obviously homemade, which always made one stand out in adolescence. There are a couple of photos of me wearing it, along with a baby-blue turtleneck and light brown cords. I chose to wear it in my regular clothing rotation. It wouldn't be until I was an adult that I would realize the gift of the outsider reveals itself in writing and in resilience that I would draw upon when coming out.

Shortly after coming out, I was on a walk with my father through our suburban neighbourhood in Kingston Township. This was at a time when, although it was legal to be homosexual and our first elected member of federal Parliament, Svend Robinson, had just come out, it would still be many years before our relationships were legally recognized and health benefits could be shared with same-sex spouses. It was a sunny, bitter cold day and we walked along the shore of Lake Ontario. The winter waves were crashing in against

the ice at the shore. My father said, "There are many others who've come before you. Oscar Wilde, Virginia Woolf, Liberace, Alexander the Great. You
are just following in their footsteps."

It took me a minute to realize what he was telling me. "Thanks, Dad,"
I choked out as warm tears flowed, then froze, down my cold cheeks. I remember the sun and my father's reassurance warming me and looking out at
that same blue sky with wonder and relief.

I still look up to that blue sky that graces us, especially in September.
My favourite view is to look up at a glacier and the aching deep-blue sky
while standing in the alpine and breathing it all in. I don't even fully understand the wonder and excitement I feel each time; perhaps it is a body memory of the deep wonder of an almost-five-year-old on the biggest adventure
of her life.

Out of the Blue

Blue diamonds sequin brittle snow,
on a winter walk with dad and dog,
not long after I'd come out.

My father, who'd expressed nothing about it,
out of the blue says,
Well, you're in good company,
there are many famous people who were gay
and he names them, has memorized them:
   Oscar Wilde
   W.H. Auden
   Alexander the Great
   Billie Holiday
   Aristotle
   Socrates
   Vita Sackville-West
   Virginia Woolf

late afternoon sun glints across that Great Lake,
rays sparkle the diamond snow,
as warmth mounts and mantles my brow.

HOME STUDY

Six days after our would-be children were born, we started our formal home-study process with British Columbia's Ministry of Children and Family Development on November 1, 2007. Back in Toronto some years earlier, we had jumped into a Dykes and Tykes course at the 519 Community Centre. We did it spontaneously, without much prior discussion, long before we came to a consensus on starting a family. It was like so much at the beginning of our relationship: jump in, be delighted, don't sweat, except about how in love we were and the impossibility of return from such a love. Nevertheless, although we had dabbled in child-rearing conversations in the past, on the other side of the country, it was tender to start the actual process all these years later. The prospect of raising children together finally got me to realize I hadn't been in the right relationship with my ex. What if that happened to Amy this time?

Amy and I scoured our list of male friends who could be sperm donors but eliminated all of them for one reason or another; that route just felt complicated. At the time, an unknown donor felt daunting with the rules in place and the fact that we lived eight hours from a clinic. Depending upon Purolator to deliver live sperm in a timely way was not our chosen path to having children. More importantly, neither Amy nor I had a strong desire to be pregnant or give birth or pass on our genetic material, for that matter; hence adoption emerged as the best fit for our own values. This was around the time that borders were closing to international adoption for same-sex couples. There were thousands of Canadian kids that needed homes and here we were, a couple who wanted kids, so we opted for domestic adoption through the Ministry of Children and Family Development.

I managed to sound calm during my initial phone call with the adoption worker. "My partner and I would like to start the adoption process."

"Please give me your and your husband's name," responded the government worker.

"Um, well, I don't have a husband. My partner is a woman," I managed to state, while my wife paced in the background.

"I'm sorry. I mean partner. I want you to know that the Ministry of Children and Family Development does not discriminate on the basis of sexual orientation," said the social worker.

Throughout the adoption process, we were told consistently that it would likely take longer to find a match for us because we were not the ideal family that many social workers or birth families imagine for adoptive children. This was always followed by an awkward explanation that the ministry was not homophobic but wanted what was best for the children in care and that it was easier to get buy-in from all parties involved with mom-and-dad adoptive parents. From our very first phone call, I was left feeling excluded and began to have concerns about the ministry's biases. Policy is one thing but anecdotes of individual social worker biases abound, from flat-out "Homosexuality is a sin" to "The ideal family is a mom and a dad."

To start the process one must engage in what is called a *home study* conducted by a registered social worker. Because the government social workers were understaffed, they contracted it out. With a shock of white in her long mane, our contract social worker started ushering us through the process full of competence and with the empathy that comes with being an adoptive mother herself.

We received the adoption packages from the Ministry of Children and Family Development with an "adoption questionnaire" that included a laundry list of characteristics and diseases that prospective families must opt in or out of accepting. We referred to it as *the dreaded checklist*. Were we prepared to adopt a child with a shortened lifespan due to degenerative disease? How about physical disability, fetal alcohol spectrum disorder (FASD)? A child born out of incest? Rape? A child with spina bifida? Neonatal abstinence syndrome? The list overwhelmed us. Unless we were open to some less-than-ideal circumstances, we were unlikely to be matched for a very long time or at all through the ministry's process. The profound joy we felt at making the decision to start a family by adoption was attenuated by the reality.

That every adopted child has special needs was burned into our psyche by the social workers. We were used to reading those words but it washed over us. We were left bewildered by this wide definition, unsure of how it would manifest. Were we taking reactive attachment disorder, developmental delay, oppositional defiant disorder? We wondered if they were just covering their asses, having heard of a high-profile case of an adoptive family relinquishing their children because they couldn't handle special needs. Was it really that common? We would soon come to understand first-hand what *special needs* can mean for kids with interrupted attachment. But at the time it was an opaque sea into which we could not penetrate until we dived into actual, real parenting.

We sat with the form for a long while. Unless we had company, it stayed out on the table so we could slowly metabolize the possibilities. We agreed each of us had veto power over any ticked boxes. I was more comfortable with physical disability, having worked in rehabilitation; Amy was more comfortable with behaviour issues. We had been told there was a trade-off between age and attachment, between diagnoses that might emerge and age. The older the child, the more is revealed in terms of medical conditions and psychosocial issues, but also the more likely there is interrupted attachment. Did we want kids who had no bonding issues or did we want kids who were old enough to be cleared of FASD? We were unlikely to get both. It was such a profound mix of emotions in the process; we were excited about moving forward in the adoption process and bewildered and saddened by the reality of adopting from the pool of BC's waiting children, of which, we were told, there were 1,300 at the time.

In the course of the home study, the social worker visited us approximately six times in our home to examine our lives. We prepared each time by dressing in casual clothing that managed to also convey success. The low-key success of wearing a nice fitted blouse or a merino wool shirt that manages to convey expensive without bragging is elevated to an art form in Nelson, with its abundance of outdoor adventure stores. Before every visit we practised answering the questions we thought would be asked. It felt as if we were selling our house, given how we cleaned it each time and served snacks. We met on our deck in fair weather. "Tell me about growing up. How is your relationship with your siblings?" asked P'nina, the social worker.

"I am very close with my brother Justin," I said. "He was born when I was eight. I was like his second mom. I carried him around, met all his needs. Although he lives in Thailand, we remain very close."

"What about your other brother?" asked P'nina.

"Well, where to start? James and I aren't close, never were. I was an only child for five years. I remember him always being a difficult kid. And it got worse from there."

During the next visit we walked through our house counting fire extinguishers and smoke detectors. The whole process ran the gamut from mundane to intrusive.

In decriminalizing homosexuality, Prime Minister Pierre Trudeau stated, "There's no place for the state in the bedrooms of the nation." It was to go against the grain, then, to invite "the state" into our bedroom. I felt guarded knowing the history of discrimination against our people. Were we intimate? If so, how often and was our sex life healthy? Had either one of us had an affair? So unaccustomed were we to answering sex questions, so hyperaware of societal discomfort, that it was an uncomfortable leap to now be talking openly about our sex life with a heterosexual social worker. And the slightly less but still uncomfortable "How do we deal with stress and conflict?" It was a revelation to see our milestones recorded in this way.

Social workers with children to place comb the home studies for matches for their kids. Ours said, "Loving home, active, outdoorsy, social drinkers, like to travel, spiritual but not religious. Have means to look after children. Both professionals. Have both dealt with difficult life experiences, and have healed things well including going to counselling." I was moved by the observation that we had a lot of strengths as a family. I was learning to see my challenges not in terms of them happening but in terms of my handling them well—a new awareness of my resilience perhaps.

In some ways I think it is easier for LGBT folk to go through this process because they don't assume that they can have a child without some sort of intrusive procedure. It was an advantage. An advantage for us was that we weren't grieving infertility. We wanted children, there were thousands who needed parents and we felt strongly that bringing more children into the world was not an ethical choice for us. Adoption was our chosen path from all the options, not the option we were left with. There would be enough loss later on.

My partner got flagged in the home-study questions around substance use, specifically her drinking habits during college. She was realizing she was gay in the midst of a small college-town scene rife with frat parties and overt homophobia. Alcohol cushioned that discomfort and masked the trauma of coming out to parents who were afraid of what she had become and the bad "choice" she was making to be gay. It was the only flagged concern of our application. I could have easily been categorized the same way but for some reason this wasn't noted by the social worker. I would guess many LGBT people who are coming out drink too much in the early days or did so when acceptance was more of a gamble, when the threat of job loss was real. Not that I'm advocating alcohol as a good coping mechanism. Still. Obviously we made the cut; there were no major stumbling blocks from the home study. It said, "Jane and Amy have come to a place in their hearts and relationship where they are ready to parent a child together. They thoroughly enjoy the time that they spend with their nieces and nephews and with children of their friends; however, they also find there is a deeper yearning to share their love, the security of their relationship and home and their hearts with a child on an everyday basis." This description, while flattering, sounded more rational than we ever were. I don't know how else a social worker could have expressed it in a way that would make us strong candidates. I think she did an excellent job.

At the same time, we were doing a weekly course with other prospective adoptive parents. This had to be done by teleconference because of the geographical challenges of our remote and dispersed region, with prospective Kootenay parents within a four-hour radius. The course dealt with an array of issues, including the dreaded checklist. In the course we discussed how to deal with curious onlookers as newly adoptive families and how to respond when someone asked, "Who is the real mom?" It was our first glimpse that we had already built up some good resources from coming out and taking our place in the world, that within our earlier despair or struggle were sown the seeds of our resilience.

During this waiting period—besides watching the seasons pass and trying to enjoy our numbered days of relative freedom to hike and get outdoors—we attended a workshop for prospective adoptive parents in Nelson. I remember listening with alarm to an adoptive parent who was a featured speaker. "I will always remember the first time my daughter referred to me as her mother. She painted her wall with 'My mother is a fucking bitch.'" I turned toward Amy, who was beside me. A look passed between us that said *Can we do this?* Amy squeezed my forearm. We resumed listening to that courageous woman. "I am grateful that my daughter finally called me her mother. This was progress for a kid who was so hurt." This story was both sobering and also an opportunity to check in about rising to the challenges of adopting children. I convinced myself that our path would not be so rocky. I was never under any illusion that family life was all sunshine and roses, so in the end I was moved but undaunted.

Now, as a parent, I understand how much that mother must have distilled her heartache to be able to recount that story with a smile in front of our group.

Our home study was finally finished and put into the Ministry of Children and Family Development system in July 2008. We got a call from a social worker, Janice, in late August asking us to meet with her to review the information. She spent an inordinate amount of time asking us about our willingness to adopt twins, noting that we hadn't ticked that box on the form. I turned to my partner, the original impetus behind not checking the box, because she was freaked out by the twin girls in *The Shining*. Not having seen the classic flick, I was wilfully naive and had no problem with twins but I was overruled when we originally filled out the paperwork. When we realized this wasn't just a theoretical question, Janice, with a glimmer in her eye, confessed, "There are boy-girl twins that a social worker from elsewhere was considering you as a prospective match for."

"Are you serious?" we both asked.

"So, are you interested in hearing more?" she said. We looked at each other and nodded our heads enthusiastically.

"They are biracial, Indian Caucasian. They are gorgeous and ten months old." We hung on every word. "There is something else. They are placed with an evangelical Christian foster family." She paused.

"What does this mean for us?" This freaked us out.

"I'm not sure. I will put your names forward with the adoption social worker."

We walked out agog, I suppose like a pregnant couple staggering out of an ultrasound that confirmed twins, but, it being the first trimester, understandably cautious. And the evangelical curveball had us wondering how much influence foster parents had over choosing a suitable adoptive family. It was so much information all at once.

Biting Buttons

In grade three I lived in a new suburb in Streetsville, which has since been swallowed up by Mississauga, Ontario. The houses are modest by today's standards but seemed large to me, coming from a two-bedroom apartment in a four-storey walk-up at Yonge and Highway 401 with the constant whine of trucks and cars on the expressway. The new subdivision, brick-facade backsplits, semi-detached and, the most coveted, two-storey detached, were inhabited by people clawing their way into the middle class, construction labourers and T-fal saleswomen, or new immigrants with dreams that would take many of them beyond this modest subdivision. We were there thanks to public mortgage insurance for first-time homebuyers, since my parents couldn't afford the 25 percent down payment required in those days. My father had a secure job at Ontario Hydro at a time when Canada's appetite for electricity was growing and needed to be fuelled with domestic raw materials. In his case, working at a coal-fired generating plant helped too, given the OPEC oil crisis.

All the kids from our neighbourhood walked to Vista Heights Public School. It seemed a long way up the dirt hill at the perimeter of the subdivision, but the fact that we walked home for lunch meant it couldn't have been more than ten minutes each way. A fallow field lay on the other side of the dirt path, probably sold to a developer by a well-off farmer. The fertile Credit River valley had no business being subdivided into house-sized lots or, for that matter, being taken from the Huron people, who were relegated to less fertile land, their Indigenous ceremonies diminished to an annual Bread and Honey Festival in Mississauga. We played in the construction zones, skeletons of houses, until adults told us not to. *Danger,* they said. But it was fun to jump through second-storey two-by-four-framed walls to the dirt basements or out of the empty window frames to the long-grass remnants of fields.

I walked back up to school after lunch with my friend Nancy. Brock, twin brother of bad-boy Brent, joined us. Brent approached me, got in my face.

"Girls aren't as strong as boys."

"Oh yeah? Are too."

"Are not."

"Are too." He got closer with each refrain. I didn't back down. He pushed me in the chest and cuffed me with his whole arm.

"Oh yeah? I'll show you." I punched him as a crowd gathered around us. Most were on my side. Brock, the nice twin, was yelling, "Brent, stop. You shouldn't hit girls."

"What is going on here?" Mrs. German, our no-nonsense grade-three teacher, bounded over and through the rowdy crowd. "Stop it. Break it up!" Before she got there, I bit my own buttons on my blouse. I bit one of them off completely and the other was misshapen and had teeth marks. I'm ashamed to say I did this to ensure he would get in more trouble than I did. I mostly got off scot-free but Brent got detention because boys weren't sup-posed to hit girls. While I generally support that rule, I know it came from an assumption that boys were the stronger sex and girls weaker. As if girls' ire couldn't be taken that seriously. Whatever I lacked in upper body strength, I made up for in ferocity. I don't recall my parents' reaction but I don't think I got in much trouble at home either. We were left to work these things out, mostly. Each day we had copious amounts of unsupervised time with friends, including the walk to school. It was the times but it was also that my mother was at home alone with a difficult toddler, James, the eldest of my younger brothers. He peed on neighbours when they visited and smeared his feces on the walls, behaviour my mother was understandably overwhelmed with. And this, while my father worked all the overtime he could in addition to his shift work as an electrician. The overtime was motivated by my parents' desire to dig themselves out of a financial hole they had found themselves in when my father went on strike just months after we bought the house. The strike and the expense of our plane tickets back to England, after my maternal grand-father died, had resulted in a pileup of debt.

❦

In trivial matters, like a fight with a classmate, I vocally and vehemently defended my position, hoping to be seen and believed. Yet when my friend's older brother sexually abused me over a period of months when I was eight and nine years old, I was silent for nearly a decade. He made me promise not to tell and besides, I didn't think my parents would believe me. Because I chose to return to the perpetrator's house to see my friend, I somehow bought that it was my fault, even though he used his lacrosse stick to violate me. My mother used to complain about me hanging out with that particular friend because Nancy was always late. She asked me to come home for lunch rather than going to Nancy's, because we were often late returning to school in the afternoon. Perhaps it was my mother's instinct that there was some family dysfunction, though she never would have dreamed to what extent.

It was not until I was sitting in a York University dorm, while at badminton camp, that I told some friends in a roundabout way. Their only qualification was that they were teammates and shared a dorm room with me, and we were far away from home. "Have you ever had sex?" one of them asked.

"I have," I said.

The most thoughtful and healthy of my badminton friends asked, "How young?"

"Eleven." I remember saying this because I knew that "having sex" was not what happened at nine years old. This was a story I could live with at the time but it further ingrained my shame.

She asked, "Did you tell anyone?" Silence hung in the dark, stuffy air in our dorm room.

"No."

I told myself this story, that it wasn't assault, for a long time.

In the American poet Frank Bidart's poem "Confessional," the guilt in both the title of the poem and the poem itself arises from collusion. Collusion gives way to the forbidden, and the response to the forbidden is silence. His poems from *In the Western Night* deal with this collusion in a way that offers no triumph over damage or shame and, hence, no respite. The poems instead offer only witness and speak to me deeply. The thing that continues to damage is that I didn't feel safe to tell my parents, didn't think I'd be supported, felt as if it were somehow my fault and felt utterly alone.

My fear came out in other ways. "Dad, I can't sleep. Can you read me a story?"

"Okay, one."

When the story was finished, I said, "Read me another." My dad, tired after a long workday, turned to leave my room. "I'm scared."

"There is nothing to be scared of. Don't be silly."

"I'm scared of something under my bed." He would check and reassure me it was clear. Still, I wouldn't get up for fear of my legs being grabbed. But the worst fear was that I would die of leukemia. I saw an after-school TV show about a girl who did and was gripped by this fear. I never shared the terror I felt about cancer.

✦

Of sexual violation there is little to be said that hasn't already been said better by Dorothy Allison or Maya Angelou. What I can say about my story is that it was at the hands of a neighbour, my friend's older brother. I blamed myself for decades. Ironically, the lacrosse stick that desecrated my preadolescent body was what ripped a hole in my story that it was my fault and that it was just having sex young. For it is impossible to reconcile that violation with consensual sex. I could no longer inhabit that denial when I started to remember viscerally what it was like. It was in my misery, then, of the worst of the abuse, that I found the key to my healing. Still, the biggest issue was getting over the isolation of holding a secret, of believing that I was no good and that it was my fault.

In my first year of university, feeling overwhelmed and near tears, I ran across a frozen soccer field on a blasting cold night, falling into icy waves of snow created by the cruel wind. Far from my family, I was finally ready to abandon the story that I had sex at a young age and blurted out my truth in the dark to my friend Sheelah. The simmering need to speak my truth, coupled with feeling very close to and very seen by this friend, led me to this moment. Sheelah would eventually become my first girlfriend.

Relocation was my saviour and not for the last time in my life either. We moved three hours away from Streetsville to Napanee. Geography was my friend too—farmer's fields were freedom and this time there was no chance they were going to be subdivided outside of a small town in eastern Ontario. I could only wish the same for my psyche, that it would be no longer divided, but that wish would not come true until I was well into adulthood.

At the time, from nine years old onward, I did not understand my loss of innocence; I just knew that I had been involved in a devastating secret. From then on Barbie had sex in my Barbie camper and my friends thought I played weird. I ended up being kind of shunned within the Barbie universe. I recall being pretty domineering in play, needing to be in control. My other friends played innocent games at one side of the room and I played on my own with Barbie. The loss of innocence continued with slight variations in adolescence. There were boys who felt entitled to take what they thought was rightfully theirs—kisses, gropes, petting. Big, stupid farmer's kids, rutting pigs or so it seemed to me at the time. Fathers driving me home after I babysat their kids and copping a feel. I don't think I was exceptional in this way.

Teenagers Talk About Sex

I'm drawn to and dread the slumber party chatter
When was your first experience?
Have you kissed a boy, gone to second base?
Sometimes I say nothing,
because baseball is not an apt euphemism.
Other times I brag, "I had sex already" and
my thirteen-year-old friends all stop and stare.
The healthy ones cringe,
then I say, "Joking," instead of mentioning choking.
Even so they know there's something wrong,
I'm telling them my story framed in false consent.
Most of the time, even now, I keep quiet about sex,
when it started for me and what came after.

Thankfully I had sports, during which I was fierce and focused. I was often the last kid out stickhandling while skating laps on the frozen cow pond when there was no one left to pass to or shoot at. The boys had gone home because of the cold and it was often just me left to skate a few extra laps. I wanted to be number twenty-seven, Darryl Sittler, on a breakaway getting a pass from Lanny McDonald. It was the most free I felt, post-trauma. Even in my figure skates, I was better than most boys. The cold didn't matter to me once I got going, not until I had to take my feet out of my figure skates and put them in my frozen boots that had doubled as goalposts in the minus-twenty-degree-plus-wind-chill weather. On the few occasions that my brother came to hockey, I made him play net while I fired shots at him. He never wanted to play goalie but I had five years on him and he didn't get to decide.

After pond hockey, I'd tromp back across the frozen field, climb the four-foot cow fence and cross the highway to our house, spent and happy. I asked my parents if I could play on a girls' hockey team but, not being accustomed to Canadian hockey culture, they said, "No. Girls don't play hockey."

Plus it was expensive and I'd need rides to and from practice and we lived out of town.

I focused on sports that were accessible to me. Each day at recess I played basketball with the boys. This transformed into playing on the girls' basketball, volleyball, soccer and badminton teams in high school. In grade ten, I took great pride in beating one of the male jocks in badminton and watching him crumple his racket because he lost to a girl.

I earned my feminist credentials on the ground, watching the advantages boys and men were given: better playing times, more practice times, more funding for competition, praise for being physical, positive reinforcement for playing sports, often the best coaches. I felt betrayed as a girl and therefore I wanted to be a boy. At nine years old, I raked our front lawn topless, to my mother's chagrin. I was so eager to learn woodworking from my dad but he only reluctantly taught me the most rudimentary of skills, choosing instead to work alone or teach my brothers. My math teacher in grades nine and ten, greying, besuited Mr. Roth, welcomed us with a speech from his loose, mastiff-like jowl about what to expect, in which he told us that women aren't good at math. When we called him out, he challenged us to name one famous female mathematician. This only made me dig in more to prove him wrong. As for sports, the girls' basketball teams were certainly not travelling beyond their rural catchment to play but the local boys' hockey team went to Sweden on a hockey exchange. I occasionally played up in basketball, junior when I was midget, senior when I was still junior. There was an added bonus of being around older basketball stars to whom I was attracted, long before I would have ever identified it as such. I just knew I wanted to be near them.

I watch my children now. Both of them are very co-ordinated and athletic. I see them gaining confidence when they are keeping up and excelling at soccer or basketball or baseball. My wish for them is that the confidence they feel in athletics can be extrapolated to other parts of their life. It ended up being a lifesaver for me.

WHAT WILL YOU DO IF YOUR KIDS GROW UP TO BE STRAIGHT?

When we said yes to the social worker about tossing our hat in the ring for the adoption process, we were being considered along with about eight other couples initially. Every two weeks or so we got an update from the social worker stating that we were still "in," as they whittled it down to six families, then four, and so on. We were particularly nervous about this process after being told we were not a *model family* for many social workers because we were a same-sex couple. Thankfully our social worker saw beyond our sexuality, though we were asked to do a number of things that we considered extra work because of our same-sex family status—a "gay tax," we jokingly called it. Nevertheless, we overachieved when asked to write an essay on how we would provide the twins, especially the boy, with positive male role models. We hastily made a mental checklist and compiled a real list of our suitable male friends who could potentially step up for weekly play dates and mentorship opportunities. We laid out in a thoughtfully detailed essay how we would provide the children opportunities for exposure to their ethnic heritage, given that their bio-mom was originally from southern India. We planned to visit large metropolitan areas every chance we had, attend Diwali and eat Indian feasts weekly. Our willingness to jump through hoops was an advantage because we didn't assume making babies was a right, nor did we assume it wouldn't be an invasive process.

We were skeptical given the systemic biases, so we were pleased to hear from our social workers that we were one of two families still in the running after their deliberations. Being competitive in team sports, we referred to this as the finals, sudden death. The process seemed to drag on and when we pressed them on why, we were finally told it was so the evangelical Christian foster parents could meet us in person to reassure them and to help them tolerate the thought of us as the adoptive parents. We were meeting so the Christians could get to know us and ask some questions, noting that they had never knowingly talked to any "homosexuals," according to the social worker. While this was a healthy step for developing a working relationship, it further delayed things. All I wanted to do was see the little girl and boy whom we'd heard so much about and whom we wanted to adopt. I wanted to witness their every movement and gesture, knowing that, at thirteen months, they were becoming more mobile and changing so much every day. Normally this meeting would not take place. Normally we would meet the kids at the same time we met the foster parents and started the adoption transition. Janice, our social worker, called and said, "The Kelowna social workers want you to meet with the foster parents and with them to try and help this process along. Can you meet on either December 20 or December 21?"

"We fly out for Christmas to see family on December 20. Could we meet earlier?"

"No, they are the first available dates."

"We could try and change flights."

"No, don't do that. They will figure out another date."

When we got the call proposing a new date, we were walking along our main street in the snow. "They can't make it work between everyone's schedules until January 14."

Amy yelled as if in pain "No!" as she slid down the wall of a shop. Bystanders thought she was physically hurt or having some kind of attack. I crouched down and put my arm around her. I always take longer to absorb these difficult bits of news so we passed the baton of comforting the other from me to Amy as we reacted in our own ways to the news.

Eventually, we made the long, snowy drive to Kelowna to show the foster family we didn't have snakes for hair and to answer any questions they had about us. After many months of being in this process, we sat in a government boardroom with beige walls and a view of Kelowna sprawl and met with the twins' foster parents. She was soft featured, maternal and smiling; he, thin, angular and slightly combative. Both had thick Scottish accents. They sat at one end of the large table and we at the other, buffered by three social workers. It was the most important job interview of our lives. The foster parents' accents put me at some ease. Fundamentalism wrapped in a Scottish accent was more palatable to me somehow. Or perhaps it was my inclination, when face to face, to find the common ground, knowing that whatever our topical differences, we humans share many more commonalities. "So, you are Scottish?" I asked.

"Yeah, is that a problem for you?" the foster dad answered.

"No, as long as the kids aren't fed deep-fried Mars bars," I said, chuckling. "I'm from northern England and in fact my ancestors fought as mercenaries in the border wars and our family was granted the right of wearing the tartans of one of the clans."

"Which one?" asked the foster dad.

"I'm sorry, I don't remember. It's blue and yellow," I said.

"Can you tell us about the twins? What are they like?" Amy asked.

"They are cute. The boy is Mr. Energy Efficient, a little more laid back. He likes the rhythm in Indian music," the foster mom said, smiling.

"The girl is Ms. Energy. She crawls over him and steals his bottle and his blankie. They have little silky snuggle rabbits the size of face cloths. She also takes care of him," he added.

Although not relaxed, the meeting proceeded well until one of them asked, "What will you do if our children grow up to be straight?"

Amy pleaded with me with her eyes. I fielded this question. "I'm not a ballet dancer, but if one of my kids turns out to be, I'd be happy for them." I exchanged a quick glance with Amy. "Chances are they will be straight; that's totally fine. We just want our kids to be happy."

Despite the questions from left field, it was clear the foster parents loved the twins, whom they'd fostered since shortly after birth. We began to form a picture of the twins in our mind but hadn't yet seen a photo, which felt excruciating and also protective.

It wasn't made clear to us who the decision maker was and we had no idea where we stood. What if this wasn't going to work out? Little did we know we were meeting so the foster parents could get to know us and hopefully this would lead them to sanction us as parents while we overlapped in caring for the children. The social workers' alternative was to yank the children out of their home if the foster parents refused to co-operate.

After the meeting with the social workers and foster parents, we tried to hold ourselves back from getting too attached to the idea, but the reality was that we were goners. Try protecting your heart against the threat of loss when you are in love. Two pixies looking out at us from a social worker's computer, big brown eyes, little amused smiles, was the first-ever glimpse of the twins we were afforded, just after that meeting. Seeing a picture of your prospective children is a whole other reality compared with talking about their medical files and hearing a little about personalities.

On our drive out of Kelowna back to Nelson after this initial meeting with the foster parents and social workers, we stopped at a kids' consignment store. We found a double bike trailer and after protective reluctance, we threw caution to the wind and bought it. We reasoned that we would pay a premium for such an item back home, that was, if we could even get our hands on a used trailer with Nelson's competitive bargain hunting for active-wear and sports equipment. It felt risky and yet delightful. It was packed in the back of our Subaru, like a foreshadowing of packing twin car seats in the back in the not too distant future.

That long drive home also gave us time to rehash meeting the foster parents. "Did they really ask 'What will you do if your kids grow up to be straight?'" Amy asked.

"Yep, they really did," I said, shaking my head.

"And did you really pull a half-articulate answer out of your ass?" Amy asked.

"You tell me. They are just expressing what others quietly fear, that we can determine our children's sexuality. Why do people dress their girls in pink and boys in blue? Why do they tell boys not to cry?" I asked from my soapbox.

"I always think of the brilliant line in the '90s movie *Leaving Normal* when Christine Lahti is staying in a kid's room, adorned with hockey and aviation memorabilia: 'Oh my God. This room has "Please, God, don't make my son a fag" written all over it.'"

"Ha, exactly! You are always good for a movie quote," I said.

Days passed during which we busied ourselves with distractions, held back from hounding the social worker and tried to be subtle in our baby-proofing efforts. It was a mind bender to see our house through the lens of possibly sharing it with twins any day now. The step down into our living room from our kitchen, once charming, was now a hazard; the corners of our coffee table didn't even register but were now a potential head-bashing weapon; and the electric outlets, once benign, were another source of worry.

When the phone call finally came, I was standing in the kitchen staring at the call display, scared and excited. "Are you sitting down?" Janice asked, in a trying-to-be-professional-but-excited voice. I called for Amy and put the phone on speaker, for I knew this was it: we'd either be told we were a match or not. Our dream come true or our bubble burst. "You have been matched with the twins. We'd like to know if you want to adopt them."

We beamed at each other while sitting on our stools at the island, having obeyed Janice's direction to sit. "No way. Oh my God. That's amazing. Okay, what happens if we say yes?" I said, the rational part of my brain kicking in.

"We'd like you to give us an answer within a day or two. We need to start this process as soon as possible. You will be over at the foster parents' home for about two weeks."

"We have to *live* with the foster parents?" I blurted.

"You won't stay with them but will be with the twins for every waking hour so they can get used to you and so you can learn their routines. You will stay at a hotel nearby. Normally this process is done by having gradually longer visits and them staying with you for a few days at a time, but given how young they are and that it's a five-hour drive away, we think this would be the best."

We got off the phone and hugged. I also recall noticing how quiet our home was, how everything was in its place.

The news we received set in motion two weeks of frenzied nesting, what most couples have nine months to do. We looked for cribs and managed to find two used ones. We researched strollers, decorated the children's room with sweet borders of multicoloured balloons and stocked up on baby supplies. Our complete lack of knowledge about diaper sizes and what clothes they needed curtailed our excitement and our tendency to want to shower them with special everything.

Tolerance

Cat fears dog before they meet.
Soon dog lunges towards cat asleep.
Cat hisses, stands tall. Deluded dog
resumes chase 'til cat scratches its snout.

In time, dog may see the curve of tail
the yellow eyes, the stubby nose as cat
not threat.
Cat, too, may curl up closer to dog's sun-drenched fur
when there is no other warmth in the old house.

I Came Out of Her Womb

At 2:00 a.m. on May 26, 1966, I came out of Patricia Anne Byers's (née Low) womb. I was a honeymoon baby and premature so people talked when I was born by C-section seven months after my parents' wedding night. Or perhaps they would have talked if my mother and I hadn't almost died in childbirth. I went without oxygen for a few minutes and the doctors told my mother not to expect much. She was nineteen and had to process the information that I would likely need institutionalizing. Although she was too sick to see me for days or hold me for weeks, she described our reunion as joyful. She had eclampsia and then the Rh factor in our respective blood was not compatible. This caused a difficult birth during which she lost a lot of blood. She was transfused with the wrong blood type, which almost caused her demise. Perhaps my mother's and my closest moments have been rare heart-to-hearts about how I came into this world. I feel some sort of weird pride at being a survivor from day one, but sadness emerged as I read about attachment in preparation for adopting our twins. What would it have been like for a newborn to be alone in her incubator, not held by her mother? I can only really access this sadness by proxy, by feeling sad for my own kids, who were taken from their birth mom as soon as they were born.

When my mother recovered, it was back to selling fresh produce in their greengrocery shop in Haslingden, a view of the treeless green hills of Lancashire out the front of the shop, while my father, Alan, worked at the large television vacuum tube factory, Mullard's, a thirty-minute bus ride away in Blackburn. My father then relieved my mother in the shop in the evenings. When I wasn't in the shop with my mother, my paternal grandmother looked after me a lot. I was the apple of her eye and she shone me up. My mother wanted this role, I can tell, by the way she recounts those times.

If you saw my mum and me side by side, you wouldn't know we were related. She: bleach blond, petite, usually in high heels, makeup. Me: solid build, not petite in any way, short grey hair, comfortable shoes, no makeup. We have very little in common in the world, except our left-wing views and our unexplained olive skin. We have our hearts, too, which are strong and full of compassion. I wasn't the girl my mother thought she wanted, we fought a lot when I was growing up, and my tomboy ways were not exactly celebrated, but I have a hunch she wouldn't trade me in. She wants me to live closer and wanted me to reconcile with my brother James, five years my junior, from whom I am estranged. At least she did want this before her relationship with James ruptured as well. For my part, I'd like it if she lived closer and had had my back a little earlier on. But this life is a drama, not a comedy: you get what you need, not what you want.

For her birthday, I once bought my mother a ceramic fire-truck piggy bank. The water tank on the bank was inexplicably shaped like a tomato and painted a faded red, as if it were anemic. My father must have taken me to the store and let me choose it, though he paid. "Oh my! This is lovely," my mother said. "Thank you. I love it." She displayed it in the centre of her dresser. I was proud that I had picked it out. I am grateful for this reminder of my mother being kind and seeing the gift, however ugly and weird it was. It occupied her dresser for a decade, from when I was about seven to seventeen years old or so. In this way, the ceramic tomato fire truck was a gift she gave me, its presence reminding me that I was loved and appreciated.

I got very ill in grade ten. My usual athletic, energetic self was laid flat in bed. I overheard my mother complaining on the phone to her friend, "She's been home for days, not getting up, being lazy. She needs to get back to school." I put my head back on the pillow, too exhausted by fever and betrayal to mention it to her when she came into my room after her soap was over and said, "Need anything? It's time you got up."

I'm not sure what daily routines I interrupted for her, besides soap operas, cleaning house and making dinner. I recall only being in bed but perhaps I was also up and needing her. Eventually she took me to the doctor and I was diagnosed with pneumonia. I think she felt badly about resenting me and I do recall getting treated with more empathy after that. Perhaps she felt badly about smoking in the house too because I think she stopped doing it for a while, but maybe she just closed my bedroom door or maybe I'm just telling myself a story to make myself feel better.

We grocery shopped weekly, my mum with my two younger brothers and me in tow. This couldn't have been easy, I realized years later, when grocery shopping with my twins. After the weekly shop, my mum would look at her grocery receipt, including the savings from coupons and sales, and if she approved, she would sometimes say, "We have a bit left over. Let's go for chips and gravy."

We would walk into the mall to Paul Bunyan's, a mediocre restaurant that nevertheless felt like a treat. "Can we have Sprite?" Usually the answer was yes, as long as we shared.

Ordering was always this weird interaction; my mother meekly ordered the french fries as if she was ashamed. It was always a male waiter. "What can I get you?" he asked.

"I don't know. I think we'll have the french fries, please." She knew; why did she feign uncertainty?

"Gravy with that?"

"Um, yes. Please." Always less confident than she was on the inside. As if wanting something definitively were beyond her. If she asked for what she really wanted, she might not get it. My mother smoked while we waited for our shared fries. The plate would be clean in a matter of a few short minutes. We could never initiate this french fry outing, because that would have meant we expected it. I am a little too much like this with my kids now. I don't want them to feel entitled to treats, yet I want them to feel entitled to take up space in the world. Not too much space, just the right amount.

On one of our weekly drives home from grocery shopping, my mother pulled over to pick up a hitchhiker. It turned out to be a woman and her children. The bitter cold flooded into the Buick as she got me to open the passenger-side front window from the shotgun position I occupied. "Where are you going?" Mum asked.

"Bath."

"It's cold. Get in." The woman and her eldest child displaced me in the front seat and I moved to the back seat along with the younger child and my two brothers. This was before anyone wore seatbelts and the massive back seat of our large sedan easily accommodated four or five kids. "We can drive you there." Bath was a village about twenty minutes out of our way and we were only driving fifteen between the grocery store and home. "Cigarette?" my mother offered. Double the usual amount of cigarette smoke choked the air and the squeak of the woman's leather jacket on cold vinyl seats was imprinted on my mind.

As we approached the village on the shores of Lake Ontario, my mother asked, "Where are you going?"

"Anywhere here is fine." She pointed to the sidewalk that skirted the park. The waves off Lake Ontario were bashing the dock.

"We're here already, may as well take you where you are going."

Reluctantly, the woman said, "Millhaven." I can't remember if I exchanged looks with my younger brothers but the woman's kids avoided our eyes. I can't recall meeting my mother's eyes in the rear-view. Probably not; large sedans were not made for small mothers to see well. We pulled up to the Millhaven penitentiary; the guards had their rifles pointed our way from their towers as we stopped the car. The woman said, "My husband, the kids' father, gets a weekend pass for visits. They have a family trailer."

My mother smiled and said, "I hope you have a good visit with your husband." The heavy doors of our car slammed shut.

"Why is their dad in jail? Why do they visit him? Why is she still married to him?" came the barrage of questions from James, Justin and me.

"I don't know. Maybe he gives them money. Millhaven is a place for murderers, not just petty thieves. I wonder what he's in for?" my mother said. My brother James, sitting beside me, had by then figured out how to steal penny candy from the drunken shopkeeper of the convenience store and sell it at school. Would he wind up in prison? I kept that question to myself.

My teenage years were a tumultuous time for my mother and me. While this is not uncommon, the particulars of my experience seemed to rest on my mum resenting me for having opportunities, such as playing sports and access to education, that she did not have. I returned from practice to hear my mother say, "Where the hell have you been? You should be home helping me make dinner, helping with your brothers."

"I was at basketball practice. There is more to life than helping you."

"Do you think I like this? Don't you think I'd like to be out cavorting?"

"That's your problem, not mine."

"You entitled bitch. We do everything for you."

"You are the fucking bitch!" I screamed as I retreated to my room. My father intervened. Ushering my mother to her room and me to mine, he would say she shouldn't yell like that and urge me to stop saying such mean things. I cringe now at calling her a *fucking bitch*. I also called her out on her anti-feminist, women-shouldn't-be-paid-equally stance. I stand by this position but not the self-righteousness. I'm getting my own comeuppance with my daughter, whose attitude has already ramped up to full-on teenager at only twelve years of age. I feel ashamed when I catch myself raising my voice and calling her entitled too.

My mother, Pat, started working outside the home when all three of her kids were in school. At first she worked part-time in retail sales before getting promoted. She organized a union at her workplace. She eventually worked her way up to full-time manager of menswear and assistant store manager at the Bay. Pat found she was very good at her job. It seemed she was much happier having a purpose other than watching and supporting the rest of her family as they lived their lives. The income helped ease some of the financial stress my parents seemed to endure as well.

When I was in my early thirties, I invited my parents to a counselling session with my therapist. I wrote them first, explaining that I had been sexually abused and that I wanted to talk to them about this with the help of a counsellor. My parents drove from Kingston to downtown Toronto. I waited with my therapist, nervous that they wouldn't come, nervous that it would go off the rails. They came. My counsellor set the stage for a nurturing conversation. "Jane wants to talk to you about what happened. This isn't about blaming anyone."

"You know I was sexually abused because I wrote it in the letter. It was hard but the hardest was not feeling I could tell you. I felt so alone for years," I sobbed.

My mother listened and wept. "I'm sorry. I'm so sorry I wasn't there for you." It was a profound moment in our relationship. We hugged and wept. It was a moment I realized I had waited many years for. Beautiful tender wreckage. My father listened and wept but said little at that session.

Afterwards, although I was emotionally spent, my therapist asked me to stay for a few minutes. She asked, "How do you feel?"

"Relieved to have said what I needed to say. Happy that my mother acknowledged my aloneness. I thought they both showed up emotionally."

"Your mother, in particular, was so present. I don't think that could have gone better. Your parents both have a lot of shame, your father especially. You did a great job. You need to be kind to yourself over the next few days." I took the streetcar home, exhausted but marvelling not only that the sky had not fallen but that they were able to be present. I wondered if the source of their shame was not being there for me. I also know the class system imposes shame and I remain forever grateful my parents made the choice to emigrate to Canada.

Brené Brown says shame is "I'm not good enough" and if you manage to get past that voice it says, "Who do you think you are?" This was my inheritance. Decades before TED talks were a thing, I hauled myself to therapy once a week. I went because that critical voice was killing me. My mother knew harshness as a survival tool, passed down through the workers' row houses that backed onto the red brick factories of the Industrial Revolution that once housed cotton mills.

Though both my parents could be kind, there was little room for the kindness or empathy of Mr. Rogers from our TV routine as kids. He ended every show with "You've made this day a special day, by just your being you. There's no person in the whole world like you, and I like you just the way you are." My mother used to say, "He's such a goody two-shoes." I quickly learned to bury any good feelings I got from watching Mr. Rogers and instead mocked him too. "Goody two-shoes," she would later say to me when I got good grades in high school and it was apparent I had my sights set on university.

When I went off to university, my parents, my youngest brother and my two best friends drove me from Kingston to Waterloo in our blue shag-carpeted Ford van with the silver lightning bolt painted on the side. We later coined it the Fuck Truck. My friends helped cushion my mother's resistance to my going away to school. I think she was afraid I would never return, and I didn't really. My father cried when we said goodbye. I eventually came to know they were proud of me when, home from university, I'd hear it from their friends at Christmas parties.

After finishing high school at sixteen years old, Pat got a labourer job at Mullard's, the large factory in her hometown of Blackburn. They made vacuum tubes for Philips TVs. Her sisters and some of her brothers worked there and she would eventually meet her future husband, my father, there as well. Advanced schooling simply was not an option for the working class at that time. Also, she was expected to earn her way as the youngest of eight children.

My mother will still occasionally grumble that too many people go to university and that trades are not as respected as they should be. I hear it as failure, for while my work is admired, it is not understood or held in as high regard as a trade or "real work," i.e., manual labour. Beneath all of this is the accusation from high school days that still stings: "You are a snob." This from my mother because I didn't talk to my brother's friends in the hallways. "Do you think you are better than them?" I was unable to answer this question for another decade and then I finally faced the voice in my head that berated me as *not good enough*. The reason I didn't talk to his friends was in fact the opposite of my mother's accusations. I was sure they didn't want much to do with me; the gulf between my brother and me was so wide at that point.

It takes many acts of small courage to follow your own wisdom, to make small changes that disrupt and then open up your life. After already following my father to a foreign land, my mother then moved to the country-side in support of my father's dreams. The large food garden demanded my mother's daily attention for rock removal, weeding, watering and harvesting, while my father worked shifts at the hydro plant. After seeing her cement backyard that was the size of a postage stamp with the stench of outhouse where she grew up, I realized it must have felt surreal for her.

What didn't seem like work was harvesting the raspberries my mother asked me to pick so she could bake pies. She, who had to that point made only meat and potato pies, started making raspberry pies and they are still my favourite. I haven't had one in years. Some of them were very tart as she learned to make them. Where did she get that recipe? I don't recall any rec-ipe books except those that came with kitchen gadgets. The electric frying pan may have had a small cookbook that described frying various meats. Recipes were handed down, which is why, except for curries, we ate mostly a traditional northern English diet growing up, though it could be argued that curry is part of that English diet and in fact has saved the English diet from itself.

The pinnacle of my mother's culinary skills was roast beef and York-shire pudding. Every Sunday the smell of slow-roasting meat filled the kitch-en. We always had Brussels sprouts, mashed turnip and carrots as well. In winter, the windows were opaque with condensation from all the boiling of vegetables. This large Sunday meal was her pride, specifically her puffed-up, airy Yorkshire puddings. She had dedicated muffin tins that were shiny and black with baked-on remnants, for those tins could never be scrubbed, only rinsed. To this day she makes it when we return to visit, still in her dedicated Yorkshire pan, despite her downsized apartment. My kids also love Yorkshire pudding with gravy, though I still have an avoidance reaction to doing the dishes after such a large meal, especially when my memories are filled with my brother James's refusal to help and my eventual giving up and getting all the dishes done alone or with the help of my much younger brother, Justin. It seemed like it took hours, the roasting pan replete with baked-on drippings and burnt bits of roasted potatoes that always needed to be soaked.

These days, I make spanakopita for my mother. She requests it on every one of our far too infrequent visits. My last few visits when my dad was still alive, I focused on making soups and dal for him. My mum was grateful for the respite after being exhausted from caring for my dad, who was very sick.

I have learned the power of withholding. I don't share things that I feel conflict about in my life, don't ask for advice on difficult life decisions and probably appear more confident than I am with her. I know it mars our relationship, but I find it easier to withhold authentic feelings with my mother. After all, I felt alone and got the message that she wouldn't *be there*. It is difficult to show her my vulnerability and though I understand what has led me here, it makes me sad.

We've made each other cry, my mother and I. We love each other. She is very proud of me, a fact she tells her friends, if not me, directly. I see her kindness with my kids, her empathy with her volunteer work at a soup kitchen. She is always making meals or tending pets of others in her building. We have invited her to visit and encouraged her to consider moving to Nelson. She is afraid of leaving her community behind. She has said she can't abandon the home and the memories she shared with my father.

BAPTISM BY FIRE

As Barack Obama ushered in a new era, making his inaugural speech as the first African-American president, we commenced fourteen days of hard labour at the foster parents' house. We were the babysitters that night, as far as the kids were concerned. Except we weren't. I cried when the twins, whom we would soon rename Franny and Theo, toddled over, a toy and a blankie in their hands to give to us. We took pictures of these slobbery, teething, spunky live wires. I laughed as the girl stepped off the couch expecting Amy to catch her, giggling all the while, and the boy crawled up to lie on me. I fell in love.

This babysitting gig kicked off fourteen days of birthing ourselves as their parents at the foster parents' home, getting to know the twins' routines and personalities and gradually taking over all aspects of their care. Sanctioning is a big part of why we had the overlap, so the kids, not yet verbal, could see the foster parents giving us permission to parent. The foster parents were present for all of it, for there was nowhere to get away in this very small house. All the while, the kids would eventually bond with us and hopefully come to think of us as safe and familiar. Over those fourteen days, they came to follow us around like ducklings imprinting on what was near. Sometimes it was fun; it felt like we were playing "parents." Other times we felt particularly under the microscope, more than just anyone would have been because we were a same-sex couple.

Our most difficult moment with the twins during this time came when we gave them their first bath alone. We had worked up to it, doing other, easier tasks with them: feeding, dressing, playing. Then it came time for us to bathe them one evening before bed.

"Mom and Mama are going to give you a bath. Make you all clean." The twins' eyes told the story of how stressful this was for them. We met their worry with smiles and calm at first. "It's okay, we've got you. I'm going to wash your body. Where's the ducky? Can you find the ducky?" As if bits of coloured plastic would distract them from the despair of having two near strangers bathe them.

"*Uuuunt*," said one of the twins. They both squirmed and cried.

"How are we going to wash their hair like this?" Amy asked.

"Let's just get it done. An express wash," I said. It escalated to terror. In hindsight, this was probably a mistake, to plow through. They sputtered and screamed and tried to stand up in the bath, while we put baby shampoo on them. We quickened our pace as they stiffened. "This is too much." But by then they were lathered and needed rinsing.

"It's okay," Amy cooed fruitlessly.

We carried them into the living room. "There, it's done. You're okay. There's Nana and Papa." I tried to calm myself. The foster parents were visibly relieved that the kids were calming down. To their credit, Nana and Papa sat in the living room and offered advice only if it was requested. Hearing the cries of the twins with no relief, despite our at-first calm, then frantic efforts to soothe them, must have been excruciating for them.

Now, on good days, I stop trying to accomplish the immediate goal in favour of the larger endgame of helping them through trauma, via calm abiding, as we had to do on a trip to the tropics recently.

Upon collapsing on the hotel bed just after arriving home from dinner, Franny was bitten by a mysterious flying beetle. She was screaming and crying at the sting and flailing her lanky eleven-year-old body around the room. We tried to comfort her as we watched helplessly while the bite swelled to a bad mosquito-bite proportion on her ankle. It was her brother, though, who went nuclear.

"We need to leave this hotel right now!" Theo commanded.

"Theo, honey, it's okay. We will make sure there are no more beetles in the room. Look, Mama is shaking everything out," I said.

"No. I hate Costa Rica. I'm not staying here," Theo said.

"It's okay. Why don't you sit with me while Mama makes the room safe? She'll shake out all the bedding."

"I will smash the TV and windows and wreck this room if we don't leave right now."

His eyes, dark terror, were the same as his eyes during that first bathing attempt at the foster parents' almost ten years before. Our efforts to console him were almost futile until, exhausted, I lay on the bed with him on top of me, making sure his body did not touch any part of the sheets or blanket, while my wife checked every inch of the room, shook out the sheets and eventually declared the room safe. He stayed on me for an hour or so, crying and calming as I massaged his back and, hoping he'd regulate with my heartbeat as he used to as a baby, whispered, "It's going to be okay. You are safe. I've got you." You would have thought that it was he and not his twin sister that had got bitten, perhaps a testament to how connected they are.

Eventually he fell asleep, after which my wife and I crawled into bed and wept too at the expressway to trauma that he found himself on. "I don't think we could have done anything any better. I mean, you scoured the room. I held him," I said.

"It's so hard. That was horrible. Is he making progress?"

"He didn't destroy anything."

"He let us comfort him." We wrapped ourselves in this thin reassurance but our hearts were a little bit broken. We cleared our schedule the next morning, opting for hangout time at the hotel pool. Everyone was tired from the unbidden adventure and we felt that having some down time without taxing the twins on another outing in this adrenalin capital of Costa Rica was important.

⁊

After that first bath, wrapped in towels in the living room, the toddlers started to calm down. Then they sat with Nana and Papa while we tried to gather up the pieces of our hearts as well as the strewn bath toys. It was times like this that highlighted the weirdness of this experience as the TV blared and the foster parents combed the twins' hair. Despite the necessity of this transition, we were eager to leave behind our baptism by fire so we could start our new lives as a family. Imagine living with the people who have raised your kids before you. It was such an exasperating mix of being chosen and auditioning for the parenting role all at once.

Afterwards, in the quiet safety of our hotel room, we processed the reaction of our kids to their bath. I felt a sadness, which was just the tip of the iceberg of the trauma we would soon be holding. I was forlorn that a bath, which offers such comfort to most kids, and is my solace when I'm sad or sore, was such a stressful experience for these sweet one-year-olds. We wanted so badly to gently bathe them and keep them safe and then wrap them up in warm towels and hold them, but they weren't ready to let us. The body knows vulnerability. They were fighting for their lives.

Gradually they learned to love baths. We would often each bathe with one of them, holding them close and keeping them warm. We took them swimming at hot springs when we could as well. The warm water relaxed us all and we hoped they would get used to the feeling that we would keep them safe.

There were other tense moments that highlighted the excruciating process we were all in. During one meal, Papa was watching closely, giving advice about feeding Theo and the need to wait for the fish soup to cool. Amy was listening and then eventually, when she thought the soup was cool enough, fed Theo a spoonful. He cried as the soup burned his lips and tongue. "What are you doing? I told you it was too hot," Papa admonished.

"I tested it. I thought it had cooled," Amy answered.

"Look, we've been feeding him for a year. We know what we're doing," Papa yelled.

The challenge for us was to be present for every need while navigating the land mines of a grieving Nana and Papa, whose emotions were likely multiplied by their beloved twins being parented by a lesbian couple. It couldn't have been easy. The extra challenge for Amy was not clawing her own eyes out with three cats in the house. She eventually acquiesced and got Claritin, though she hates taking medication. This allergy seemed appropriate metaphorically, her body on alert and reacting to a foreign invader.

The most surreal moment with the foster parents came in the kitchen one day when the foster mom said, "So how does it feel knowing you will go to hell because of your lifestyle choice?" I chose not to engage and instead focused on cleaning the sippy cups, while thinking up rebuttals ("Hell will be more fun"). The foster mother continued her questions from the other room.

After taking a deep breath and concealing my incredulity, I said, "I think I need to just focus on the kids. I don't think it is helpful to get into our respective beliefs."

"Oh, I like controversial conversations. I'm not trying to offend you or anything."

"I just really need to focus on the kids right now," I said as I was preparing snacks for the twins.

That comment put an already stressful two weeks over the top for me. This was definitely the lowest point in our clash of cultures. Thankfully we later debriefed with and got support from the normally unflappable adoption social worker, Ruth, who also seemed gobsmacked over the comment. The next day Ruth came to the house to reset expectations and set up a schedule and timeline for our departure. She reminded us that although this arrangement was very stressful for all the adults, it was necessary and in the best interest of the children.

To escape the small surroundings and the judgment, we suggested taking the twins for a hike. The foster mom, who regarded nature as something to be feared and avoided, suggested a walk at the mall instead, remarking that they'd never been outside in winter. We had to get away from the TV and close quarters and desperately wanted time with the twins alone, not to mention the fresh air we craved. We gave Nana a day to get used to the idea and went the following morning, which was sunny and mild for February. We hiked around their benched acreage overlooking Kalamalka Lake and walked down the adjacent country road with the twins on our backs. The fresh cool air was a balm for our stress. The twins looked like deer in headlights on that first hike. Theo soon loved it though and wanted to go in the backpack again. Franny, typically the more skeptical one early on, wasn't so sure. The foster mother gasped with relief when we returned. I don't think hiking was quite what she meant when she asked us how we felt about going to hell for our *lifestyle*.

The foster parents began to swap their beliefs steeped in stereotypes for ones based on first-hand experience. They saw us caring for the twins. They saw the children gradually coming to us for their needs to be met, and us meeting those needs at every opportunity. During the last meal we ate together in this transition, they said that they believed the children were well placed. It felt like tectonic plates shifting and a diamond of friendship started to shine from the black carbon of our beginnings.

These days, the foster parents are raising chickens and growing flowers on their sunny bench. The foster mom goes out to feed the chickens and collect eggs. I like to think that seeing the kids' smiles when we returned from our daily walks during our immersive adoption experience, and hearing them talk enthusiastically about all our hikes since then, has nudged Nana away from her fear of an outdoor lifestyle. Maybe we've had just a little something to do with that.

It seems like some sort of miracle that we get together with the foster parents a couple of times a year. They've told us that no other adoptive families have kept in touch to that extent, and they have fostered many children over the years. Our kids glow when they see Nana and Papa. They sort of function like a third set of grandparents. We are in an authentic relationship with each other.

I am delighted and surprised that Nana and Papa question things such as Christians' beliefs and behaviour. I simply didn't think evangelicals were allowed to question anything about their religion. On one of our visits, Papa said over dinner, "You guys are not professing to be religious but have committed to loving these kids. That, to me, is more Christian than what I see in most of the denomination stuff. They talk about it but you guys are actually practising the reality of what it is to commit and love people. So something is really screwed up here as far as you guys are doing it right and not saying you are and they're saying they are doing it right and they're not … obviously not."

"Yeah, killing people in the name of religion, even emotionally killing people," said Nana.

"It was a relief that we could get to know each other as human beings and what mattered to you was the kids, not what labels we are," I said.

"I love what you guys have done. It's liberating," said Papa.

"And the product is them … growing into themselves," said Nana.

The same people we most feared gave us our most beautiful gift by providing our children a loving and secure start to life. Perhaps as you read this, somewhere in the BC interior, there is a lesbian couple and an evangelical Christian couple who call each other family and consider each other friends, sharing a birthday cake and celebrating the twins they have all had a hand in raising. Thankfully we have all gotten beyond our labels.

Sweetness

My children craved sweets when they first came home.
I judged the foster mom for the candy she doled out to fourteen-month-olds.

Four years in and I read about attachment post-adoption,
how, mimicking a newborn, children crave sweets,
yearn for connection with their new parents
as they would have yearned for their mother's milk.

Redoing their beginnings,
these brilliant beings,
who'd yet to say a word,

who'd smash each other with rattles,
careen in soggy diapers.

I cursed the sweets.
Withheld them,
fed the kids irritation instead.

Dessert now deep pleasure.

THE REVOLUTION
THAT IS CHILDREN

The real baptism by fire started when we arrived home with the twins, after a five-hour drive during which we kept looking behind us, stunned to see two faces gazing back at us from their car seats, their eyes revealing a hint of shock, a hint of oblivion and a whole lot of exhausted. We learned the hard way not to feed Franny a bottle of milk while driving. A pit stop in Grand Forks had us wiping her down and changing her clothes, as well as doing our best to wipe vomit from the upholstery and her new car seat while standing out in the February cold.

Within minutes of getting home, our attempts at childproofing were proven woefully inadequate. The kids were taking what seemed like one giant step for mankind from our kitchen down into our living room. Amy was outside in the snow, crawling under our shed, picking through scrap wood to find a piece of plywood that would span our three-foot entry from kitchen to living room while I did my best to entertain the kids with anything but toddling up and down this exciting new step.

At first, we were strongly advised by the social workers to drastically limit who visited us and minimize our contact with the outside world. They suggested we do so for three or four months. When children are placed for adoption, they need to have their needs met by their new parents and we really needed to connect with our kids. They say newly adopted kids will be shopping for parents with anyone they see, so we did everything for them. We wanted them to know we were their people.

We let our friends know. It was uncomfortable for us to ask our support system not to come over when we needed their support. We yearned to share a meal and conversation and wanted them to get to know our children too. And we didn't have our family around. It feels remarkably familiar now, in the COVID-19 pandemic. The four of us and our dog in our bubble, walking in the morning and hanging out together. Sure, the kids play by themselves now and we support them with online school but still it is a familiar bubble. There has been some regression, or some checking in that we are meeting their needs. Whether it's because they can't get social needs met by peers or it reminds them of our early days together or the pandemic has left them feeling anxious and unsure, they seem to really like this family bubble. If you asked them, they might deny it.

The twins also need to have much of their days witnessed. "Watch this, Mom," Franny says as she does a new routine on the trampoline.

"Mom, see how far I can hit the rocks," Theo says as he whacks rocks into the lake with a stick he's found on our beach walk.

"Mom, can you do my homework with me?"

"It looks like you are doing fine," I say, hoping to get a few more minutes to work.

"I don't like being alone. Can you just sit beside me while I work?" Franny asks.

On one walk, the kids said "Catch me" from a granite overhang on the trail.

Amy and I gave each other a knowing look and braced ourselves for twelve-year-old jumpers. "Okay, we're here for you."

When we had just adopted the twins, this bubble made sense on many levels, especially since we could explain nothing to them. It is difficult to overstate the sensory strangeness they must have encountered in a completely new home in new surroundings, without the only parents they had ever known, their foster parents. While we did try to replicate the fish stew and oatmeal from their foster home, they had to get used to completely new smells from cooking. They had to acclimate to our unique personal odours. They had to get used to a new house with stairs up to their room and a big dog. They had to get used to the particular light that comes in our windows, different from the view over Kalamalka Lake that they had known until that point. They likely had to get used to the TV not being on and to going for long walks outside in all seasons. They had to get used to not being cared for by the only caregivers they had known, and the emotional upheaval, with no explanation of having brand new people upon whom they were completely dependent.

They had to get used to new names as well. After much discussion and checking in with the social workers, we decided to change their names. Maryann, the social worker who was most familiar with their birth mom, confirmed that their given names were not culturally significant. She thought that, given the kids' age of fourteen months, it wouldn't be a big deal to change names. I still wonder if we did the right thing. I fear it will be something they get angry with us for later. We kept their original names as their middle names in honour of their birth mom. Theo just felt like a Theo; his name felt right and once we landed on it, there was no going back. Franny's name was a little trickier because Amy and I didn't agree. The foster parents shortened her original name to Shannie and I liked this name very much. I thought of Shani Mootoo, the Canadian writer. After negotiating and compromise, we landed on Franny. The kids didn't skip a beat with the new names; this was a drop in the bucket of all the other changes.

We had to get used to what felt like an invasion of our space. There was no quiet in our house any longer, except when they slept. No getting up on a Saturday morning and donning our hiking boots and going off for a day hike. Instead, there were diapers and reading picture books and applesauce containers and breakfast smeared on high chairs, though our floor was always clean thanks to our golden retriever. Although this is what we signed up for and it held many moments of delight, it was also a profound shock for everyone.

A couple of days after we came home, the Academy Awards were on. "I'm watching the Oscars," Amy said while I tried to keep the kids busy.

"The twins have other ideas," I said as they banged on plastic musical instruments and climbed on her.

"I just want to watch this one thing. I'm a filmmaker for God's sake," she said.

"Get real. We have toddlers, two of them, who just came to a brand new home. Get over yourself." Amy stomped off upstairs, seemingly mad at me, but probably thunderstruck at how her life had changed. It just didn't matter what either one of us *wanted* at any given moment.

I took paid parental leave for nine months and then took another four off unpaid. Even with twins, paid parental leave cannot be taken by both parents consecutively, or if it is, it mustn't exceed the nine-month total entitlement, though this continues to be challenged in the courts. I am grateful for parental leave in Canada, especially compared with our southern neighbours, who don't have mandated maternity or parental leave. The first three months of paid leave, called maternity leave, is for physical recovery from giving birth. Adoptive parents weren't entitled to maternity leave, because apparently we didn't need to physically recover since we hadn't given birth. Bilateral tendonitis in my shoulders from holding two twenty-pound weights without building my tolerance with newborns would beg to differ.

No one could have prepared us for the intensity of parenting toddlers who were in shock and in completely new surroundings with totally unfamiliar caretakers. It was remarkable that they were so happy day to day. Toys in front of them, they played. A beach in front of them, they walked and dug in the sand. Still, looking back at photos, it is plain to see their shock and exhaustion. It understandably took them a long time to settle in and feel safe. Theo lay on my chest every day for months after we brought him home. Franny didn't let her guard down until her brother settled. She pushed us away frequently and connected with us only on her terms. At bedtime, I would lie there on a mattress on the floor and Franny would gradually get closer. We took full advantage when she was sick. Not that we were ever happy about fevers but they did offer us an opportunity to cuddle with her and boost her oxytocin from all that bonding, instead of her usual adrenal overload. That time we lost with them as newborns was being made up for in small part by them sleeping on us.

They typically cried only when they were tired or when they awoke in the middle of the night. What their brains must have had to take in, to integrate. It's no wonder Franny is so vigilant, that she can scan a room and know what she needs to know. It was her survival early on. Her spirited, sometimes defiant attitude comes out in different ways as she grows up. It got her through early losses and receded as she attached. As a tween, it still shows itself as defiance with homework and hatred for what she refers to as "teacher's pets." She says teacher's pets are any kids who raise their hands and try in school. At home it manifests as "I hate you. You are the worst parents." Because we give her chores. I frequently remind myself that Franny's pushing away means she feels we are solid enough to push against.

In the Irish language, the word for *doubt* means *small courage*. When we first adopted the twins, they were fierce, small packages of courage. Running to us, wrapping their toddler arms around us, keeping their hearts open despite losing everything they had known—attaching to us, loving, smiling and being present in their brand new lives. Trusting, despite the terror of being plucked away from all that they knew.

When we first brought them home, it was difficult to hold the intensity and range of emotion. We were both elated and exhausted. Franny and

Theo were inconsolable with loss and grief, having lost their foster parents after already losing their birth mom, but they also laughed every day and were obviously delighted at discovering their new worlds. Hopefully this will be an asset as they move through their lives, the ability to hold grief and joy concurrently.

The pressure of parenting instant twins and the intensity of their transition had us melting down too. Sometimes these meltdowns happened without kids around but sometimes the exhaustion and the drudgery of breaking up fights or withstanding frequent toddler tantrums were just too much. My friend Peggy walked with the children and me a lot in the early days. Her kids were in university by then and she was a calm, experienced presence for me. I remember walking on the rail trail, a gentle, easy trail built on an old railbed above town. It was a mild winter day or perhaps fall or spring. Franny freaked out and screamed and refused to budge. I said, "Get up. We're walking." She refused.

I threw my hands up in frustration. "Peggy, I don't know what to do. She is so strong headed. If I pick her up, I'm afraid she'll learn temper tantrums are the way to go."

A flash of alarm crossed Peggy's face. "Go to her," she said. "Pick her up."

I felt the tingle of shame and realization course through my body. I hastily complied. I still feel ashamed. Peggy reassures me that I was learning parenting all at once, a crash course, and it was okay. In hindsight my daughter was in some kind of trauma. Crying beyond the moment, probably needing to know I was there and was not going to leave her. There were so many moments like this, when I didn't know what to do and had to figure it out. I didn't always respond with compassion, for it is hard to conceive of that much trauma. No matter the reason, I was unkind and stupid in that moment, even though I too experienced and eventually healed from trauma and knew that it doesn't always come out in straightforward ways. In my daughter's case, it so often comes out as belligerence, especially now that she is edging close to the teen years.

The closest I've ever been to hitting my children is getting bitten on my hand and stuffing my bleeding knuckles into my daughter's or my son's mouth even further to make them learn their lesson that they can't bite. It is a moment of saying "I have the power here" and it feels awful. This is so far from our lengthy discussions in the adoption process about positive parenting. Our home study states that we don't believe in physically disciplining children.

With every step forward in the parenting journey I fall from my own ideals and high expectations.

A couple of months in, absolutely sick of cooking and cleaning, we decided to venture out for a family dinner. After twenty minutes of preparation and transitioning the kids into the car in the late-afternoon winter dark, we drove the three minutes to the Hume Hotel, the place we figured had the most chance of being family-friendly and accommodating. Two high chairs and two moms, surrounded by senior citizens on account of the early-bird dinner hour—this was just one of our training excursions in standing out. We are here!

While we waited for our food to arrive, we played with the kids and gave them tactile books and Goldfish crackers to distract them from their mounting impatience at being penned in. They were not yet talking but made lots of noises and gestures. We let them get out for a few minutes and each of them walked with one of us. Yet, by the time our meals came, they were vibrating in their high chairs; sitting still was beyond them. Getting them back in the high chair was about as easy as putting an octopus back in a cave, I imagine, but the octopi were covered in soggy crackers and smelled like they needed diaper changes. We both guzzled our beers and asked for to-go boxes. There was nothing to be done. The twins just couldn't manage another completely new surrounding, one in which they had to sit still and be quiet. We went home and ate our by then lukewarm dinners, surrounded by toddler detritus. Our longing for a meal out would have to wait. As we eventually learned, it was best done while the children were at home with a sitter, or at an outdoor café with a children's play area.

We spent hours pushing them in their double stroller. Manoeuvring a stroller in a very hilly town is no easy thing—pulling it with all one's body weight so it doesn't let loose down a slope worthy of a black diamond ski run, or two of us in full-body push mode back up the hill from the lake. We used the stroller's safety tether. All that and a dog on a leash who mostly behaved but would pull when he saw wildlife and growl when he saw men with baseball hats, a remnant from his pre-rescue days. They were safe in their little cockpit, looking out at new everything and with a protective dog at their side.

We recently revisited a spot along the Slocan River that we access first by bike on the rail trail and then by foot, walking along a soggy, grassy path across mud and onto a little sandbar in a bend in the river. The last time we were there, the kids were two years old. We had to carry them across because in spring the muddy, grassy parts become an ephemeral creek, which we forded. Once we warmed our aching feet, we lay down on a blanket while the toddlers threw pebbles and twigs into the creek. It was a moment of respite in a busy life, one of us with our eyes on them in case they ventured too close, one of us with our eyes shut. They poked cracker bits in our mouths while we lay there.

It was one of the first times we biked together and had some semblance of our former selves come alive. Sure, I had a double bike trailer attached, but I was out biking in a beautiful spot and besides, it was a great workout. It felt like we were going to be okay, like the sheer exhaustion and shock of having two toddlers arrive in our lives was not going to pull us under. We could hold and protect them along the way until they could ford their own life depths.

Now they let us love them. When tired or angry, they push us away sometimes. It makes me sad, but we try and calmly abide. Usually it works out. There have been times when both kids are freaking out and can't calm and want to lash out, the highway of terror grooved in their brains from early on. It is very rare, thankfully. Eleven-year-old physical tantrums are hard to manage. We hold them and we hold their damage. Sometimes its weight shatters us and we crawl into bed exhausted and crying or sniping at each other, before we gather the bits and sleep rearranges and reforms things.

At bedtime, Franny plays this game. "I love you more, Mom."

"I love *you* more," I say.

"Nope, I love you more."

"It's just not possible that you could love me more than I love you."

"But I do," she says with a glimmer in her eye.

"Okay, how about you get to love me more on odd-numbered days and I get to love you more on even days?" I ask.

"I guess. Okay." Letting all that love in feels vulnerable and I'm imagining she feels more control playing this "game." For her eleventh birthday she gave me a gift: she said I could love her more. It's a long way from screaming in the bath. It gives me hope.

Seeing / Being Seen

"It's okay if you get pregnant in high school. I will take care of the baby," my mother said. I was in grade ten.

I said, "Uh, no. That's not going to happen. What do you think I am, stupid?" My face twisted in disgust. I had no ability to see it was about her, not me, at that stage of my life. I viewed the teenage pregnancy option as a jail sentence. I'd never felt so alone and unseen.

I was academically driven and smart, determined to be the first one in my extended family to go to university. I was on my way to coming out as a lesbian and breaking up with my high school boyfriend because I wanted to spend more time with my friends and play sports. I felt misunderstood, but it wasn't likely about me so much as it was about her. Perhaps she wanted to mother my child because she didn't feel I let her mother me or because she felt loss with her three kids growing up. Long ago, I had learned not to need her, though I didn't know how to mother myself either. It was a black hole, which I filled with grit.

I did intensive psychotherapy in my late twenties and early thirties. It was all about seeing myself and undoing shame. I didn't know it then but healing was also necessary so I could be a loving, healthy mom. I had to mother myself first and that took a while. Healing was a privilege, though I saw it only as a burden at the time. I was with a woman who was very nurturing. She showed me what courage and vulnerability were. Kate initiated our breakup, having realized I was not in love with her. Imagine the vulnerability of thinking your mate was not in love with you and the courage it took to ask it out loud and then get both vindicated and heartbroken all in one answer. She also wanted to have children and, at the time, I did not.

In my thirties, well before I ever considered having children, I volunteered with a one-to-one mentoring program through the City of Toronto. Its focus was helping foster resilience in children from drug-involved families.

It appealed to me because of my outstanding questions about the nature of my own resilience. I hoped to foster this in another kid who needed some.

Once a week I went to Regent Park Public School and hung out with a girl who was in grade five. She had a twin sister and her mother had named them both Cassandra but called them Cassie and Sandra. Cassie was guarded and half the time I wondered if I was doing any good there. We ate lunch; often I shared mine though we were warned against this. We often went for a walk, played basketball or made art while we talked. Cassie was a good kid but already there were signs of innocence slipping away and being replaced by something more ugly. One time she told me about visiting her father in the southern United States. Her mother gave her hell because she found some money in a bus-station bathroom when they were en route and gave it back to its rightful owner. She looked to me for approval.

I gave Cassie and Sandra a bursary application for summer camp. My soon-to-be wife happened to be the director of that summer camp so there was a good chance that if they met the criteria, they would be fully subsidized campers. I encouraged Cassie to get her mom to apply. I had hopes that it would also help her mother, who was a single parent, to have a break from her kids. The kids would be exposed to new worlds where they could canoe, swim and learn leadership skills away from the swelter of a downtown Toronto housing project in July. The application was never filled out.

I think of the lunches Cassie and I spent together and wonder if they made any difference at all. I was a white woman coming from her downtown corporate job to the projects to hang out with an African-Canadian kid. I thought I had to *do* something with her every week but now I have a hunch that just showing up, seeing her and asking her about herself was the most valuable part of the exercise. I know now not to underestimate the power of just showing up and seeing another.

I'm eager and driven to *see* my kids. I reflect their stories back to them so they can make meaning in their lives. Sometimes they don't want to be seen in that way, don't want us telling stories and making meaning. They just want to be kids instead—playing, not talking. At dinner with friends recently, Theo said, "Mom, I know you are going to tell the story of how I have empathy because I helped the kindergartener."

"You are right, buddy. You do have empathy."

How do we hold the despair of our families and then the hope that it will somehow be different with our children? Do we think counselling will protect us from the same fate? Do we think we listen to our children in a different way? Perhaps because of my mother's inconsistent parenting, it seems to have been my parental mission to *see the shit* out of my children. Perhaps being seen is just another definition of loving. To love is to see and not to try to change.

Last year, I went to the library to find a book for my son. Theo is a hard worker, an abstract thinker and emotionally in tune. He often didn't want to go to school up until grade five and was not enthusiastic about reading. I found the book I'd researched, *Percy Jackson and the Olympians: The Lightning Thief*—the boy who hates school and imagines vaporizing his teachers. I had hoped this would pique his curiosity and get him excited about reading. That I went to find this book is a difference between my parents and me. I think it is unlikely my parents would have found me a book if they saw me struggling. Then again, I wouldn't have shared my struggle with them. My parents were well trained to see all children as the same; to give them any inkling they were special was to set them up for disappointment. *Special* was a recipe for creating a teenage prima donna. Row houses behind the factories where they grew up outside of Manchester were not fertile ground for individuality or hope. My mother was the eighth child in her blended family. She had a disabled father. Being seen was not something anyone aspired to. In fact, moving quietly under the radar was safer. Perhaps it was a postwar mentality; after all, it was merely two years before my mother was born that the lights were turned off nightly to hide whole towns from aerial bombing raids. Sticking out was to risk one's life.

Sometimes it feels as if I'm metric and my mother is imperial and there's no conversion chart. At times I got the impression my mother didn't like me, that I wasn't enough. I always wonder what is enough; what do I need to do to be liked? In hindsight I think it is more accurate to say she is triggered by me because I have had much more freedom and opportunity in my life.

If I were to boil it down, the difference between my mother and me is that she wants to be seen by me, and I want to see my children. I was seen by her some of the time. I found others to see me. Eventually I saw myself.

My daughter wants her own bathroom and a lapdog. She swishes around like Reese Witherspoon in *Legally Blonde*. She is the Indian Reese. She is herself. Anyone who knows me knows I'm one of the least likely lapdog owners. Franny says she can totally see me with a lapdog. It is worth saying that we have a golden retriever we all adore. I laugh off this desire for a lapdog as a child's hope. I try to usher her through the discomfort of wanting what she doesn't have. Thankfully I have some awareness of the *not enough* feeling.

My mother had a brain aneurysm. She was fifty-one years old. I got the call and my regular life was put on hold. I drove to Kingston from Toronto, wondering if I'd see her alive. She was on a neurointensive care ward but she could have been on the moon for all she knew. It was so hard to see her lying there, attached to monitors and tubes, helpless. The next morning she was transported via air ambulance to Toronto Western Hospital, where she underwent surgery to repair her aneurysm. The neurosurgeon explained that it was a large bleed deep within her brain, like a balloon popping, and that she might never recover. She was likely to have another bleed, one that she wouldn't survive without the surgery. My family, my dad, my brothers and I, sat around in the airless waiting room for hours, waiting, such a departure from my busy life. The surgery took longer than they had hoped because of the size of the bleed.

She made it through surgery. Brains defend against intruders by swelling: *Don't mess with my blood-brain barrier*, they scream, and hers was no exception. The surgeon warned us about this, that despite his using a catheter through her femoral artery and up to her brain to dispense platinum coils meant to reinforce the walls of the burst blood vessel, she still had swelling. The swelling would have been the same if she'd had the more conventional surgery in which they saw or drill through the cranium. This conventional surgery was passed over by the hotshot surgeon for the newer technique that he was pioneering in Canada. At least she still had her hair.

In neurointensive care, glass walls separated each bed but the "rooms" were not fully enclosed. Nurses were positioned down the middle of the ward, one assigned to each patient, such was the need for medical vigilance. They sat taking notes for brief periods interrupted by checking the dials, tubes and levels of the myriad machines that dwarfed each patient in this unit. My mother looked normal, especially compared with the craniotomy patients who occupied other beds. After a few days of recovery, she was well enough to be moved to a regular neurosurgical unit, where she received much less nursing attention in her drab-walled private room.

Time fragmented and family relationships gelled around only this one wish that my mother would recover. We were all so focused on her every need, whether it was giving her ice chips, massaging her legs or trying to soothe her mind that her extreme headache was totally normal. After days of not knowing her own name, she blurted out to the nurse, "So you are a lesbian." The nurse paused and then continued checking her catheter and vitals. "I see your rainbow rings." More quiet. Then she said, "It's okay, my daughter is too." The nurse flashed me the tiniest of smiles. I was so relieved that she remembered anything and amused that it was a lesbian and gay symbol. And beyond amusement, she had pronounced her daughter was gay, demonstrating acceptance where there had been some consternation. My mother had seen me. I was delighted. I wondered if it was selfish to feel delight amid this tough time. Mostly it was just relief that her brain was making connections after days of arguing with staff about what day it was and where she was, classic brain-injured behaviour.

Intensive Care

Yesterday's platinum injection offers protection
from the artery ballooning at the base of your brain.
Still, damage is done:
a chaos of blood uncontained,
your motherly eyes stray.

The nurse, a whir,
changes IVs, leans down,
checks the yellow catheter.
She dispenses relief
for your invaded cranium,
jots on your chart,
and nods in our general direction.

You remember to smile and be gracious,
but forget your name.
Recognition spreads across your face
as you look at the rainbow rings
that have escaped the collar of the nurses uniform.
"So, you're a lesbian," you say, clear as day.
The nurse pauses, rechecks fluid levels, the catheter—
hesitates,
cautious as truth colours this dingy room.

Before the reply, your shaky arm points,
"It's okay, my daughter is too," you say.
So relieved to hear you remember,
I forget my shame; begin to shed restraint.
As hope pools in the base of my brain,
we slip into intensive recovery.

My mother would undergo months of recovery. She stayed off work for two years. She couldn't go back to her pre-illness job of manager at the Bay. There was too much multi-tasking, too much interaction with other people, and people are complex. She was accommodated as a display person, what we might have called a "window dresser" in the past. She flourished there among the inanimate objects, where she could order her world and limit interactions with people while her brain continued the silent, difficult work of recovery and forging new connections to compensate for neural pathways that no longer worked. My mother could concentrate on each task with little interruption. Mannequins were predictable and they did not disagree. My mother found her way back to herself and the world in an occupation that she enjoyed. With the brain injury, which impacted the visual processing centre in her brain, she lost most of her peripheral vision. I think this may have helped with display work. She was less prone to distraction perhaps.

Since I moved out at nineteen to attend the University of Waterloo, a five-hour drive from Kingston, I have been on the periphery of her life in many ways. Her son James, who never left, is immediately in front of her. Proximity counts, especially for someone with a peripheral visual processing disorder. I'm literally and figuratively outside of her central vision.

I did have a taste of what it would be like to live without peripheral vision. In my second-ever Olympic-distance triathlon, I accidentally smeared Vaseline on my swim goggles as I was standing on the town beach in Nelson, BC, in front of my newfound hometown crowd, waiting for the event to start. It was the year I took a leave of absence from my corporate job at the City of Toronto and came to Nelson alone, three years before Amy and I made the permanent move. It was a large pat on the back I gave myself for "graduating" from psychotherapy, from all that hard work, getting out from beneath the rock of shame and silence, forgiving and mothering myself. It was also, in hindsight, me searching for alternatives to living in the big city, one step closer to living my dream.

I had swum this freezing glacial lake weekly for six weeks. Vaseline is used to insulate skin against frigid water and to protect inner thighs against chafing. But the accidental smear made it hard not to get pulled astray by the considerable current in this part of the lake that becomes a river at Nelson without constantly having to pull off my goggles. I swam "blind" for a while, using other competitors' kicks and splashes to help reassure me I was on the right course. Then I would stop and correct, all the while knowing that each correction stopped my momentum and would slow my pace.

The Vaseline smear gave me a microcosm to inhabit, a small insight, knowing well I would have fully functioning vision the second I was out of the water. It was insight into how my mother saw the world. It has helped me to understand her singular focus at times, or her ability to disregard the parts of her life in her periphery.

❧

Shortly before we moved west, Amy and I took my visiting parents to Kew Beach in Toronto. It was only a kilometre and a half from our apartment in Little India. It was a sunny day and we waded in Lake Ontario. Bella, my joint-custody golden lab, was chasing sticks. "So, Mum, how'd you like to be a grandparent some day?"

"What, are you pregnant?"

"We are checking out adoption."

"Oh, that's great. I would love it. You'll make great parents." She hugged us both, beaming. I could see her crocheting scarves and making roast beef dinners already.

"We are just checking it out. Don't get your hopes up." I worried that our tentative steps into a queer parenting group sounded more definite than we actually were about having children. Besides, I always had the urge to quell my mother's enthusiasm. It felt too vulnerable. I remember being happy that night as Amy and I debriefed.

"Why did you squash your mom's enthusiasm?" she asked.

"I guess I don't want to get her hopes up," I said.

"Then why mention it at all?"

"I don't know. We don't have much in common. I knew how happy that would make her to know."

"And you want her approval."

"Yeah, I guess so."

I have channelled the need to be seen into my work. My professional work is to objectively see, categorize and analyze physical and cognitive job demands so determinations can be made for injury prevention and return to work for injured workers. As a starting point, I often ask workers what they like about their jobs. There have been many moments of grace in the answers: a trucker telling me he loves the open road with a dreamy look in his eyes, a factory labourer who sees he is an important part of an essential process, for the first time. Sometimes they have never told anyone what they like about their jobs before and the stress eases and their faces light up. Post-shift pub banter doesn't typically include gratitude for one's livelihood. My favourite part of the work is in the conversation I have with an engaged worker who surprises with insight or who dignifies his own life in the reflections. It is the stories that shine. It is a privilege to witness another's life.

No matter how much I *see* my kids, they will not be seen by their birth mom. She knows only what we choose to write in twice-annual letters. She cannot see them because they got taken away from her. Do social workers look at the likelihood of kids being seen in their homes? Does this factor into their decisions around neglect?

What is being seen? Having someone care enough to observe who you are, what you like, what you don't like, what scares you, and hold your hand a little tighter when they do notice this? Having someone care enough to be curious? Our twins will have to deal with not being seen. It's not rejection by a mother directly. It is a mother who had her children taken away because she couldn't provide a safe home for them.

I know my mother sees me more when I reveal my vulnerability enough to let her in and now that she is in the twilight of her life. Perhaps she has more mental space or wants to connect because she is alone now that my father has died. It is hard for me to let her in. I sometimes call her with parenting issues, aware that I am testing the waters of vulnerability, but I am careful too. It is always bittersweet, this push/pull of vulnerability and self-reliance. I have had feedback from the people who are closest to me that I don't tell her what's going on, that I hold my cards close. *I'm fine. Nothing to see here. Move along, thank you very much.* That isn't a model for sustainability and I step out of it when I realize I'm trying to go it alone and struggling.

The morning after this past Mother's Day, I wrote myself back into gratitude, reflecting upon and appreciating breakfast in bed and the gifts that our twins brought to us. I reflected upon the lovely bike ride we had and the picnic on a sandbar in Kootenay Lake. That is *enough*, more than *enough*, yet, as with the sandbar, there is no solid ground beneath. Instead there is my own inner critic telling me I'm not enough. Not a good enough mom, not a good enough daughter, not a good enough writer, not a good enough partner. For much of my life, stuff disappears and things don't ever feel enough because of the hole. I would have liked some things to be different but who I am right now is beyond good. I am whole. I accept who I am. Perhaps that is the most we can hope for.

Sleepy Hollow

Every day by noon, we had been up for at least six or seven hours with the twins, never mind middle-of-the-night interruptions. At night, if one of them woke up, I would bound toward their room, virtually still asleep, literally waking up crib-side as I extracted a crying twin before the other was disturbed. To get the toddlers to nap, we'd sometimes have to drive. We'd call it "going to Sleepy Hollow." The kids thought this was an actual place. They asked about it long after regular naps were a *thing*. I had to eventually confess it was a ruse to get them to sleep. The drive itself was the purpose, not some sleepy, halcyon destination.

I'd drive the twins along Kootenay Lake, either alone or with my wife on days we could manage not to be outnumbered. Most often Theo would have drifted asleep by the time we crossed the big orange bridge, BOB, as everyone calls it. BOB connects the North Shore of Kootenay Lake with the city of Nelson, adjacent to the town beach at Lakeside Park.

On Sleepy Hollow drives, when Franny could resist slumber, she would stare at us, betrayed that she'd be on her way to sleep and we weren't doing anything to prevent it. Indeed, she acted as if we were creating the conditions for sleep. As the dying sometimes need permission to let go, she needed us to reassure her we'd still be there when she woke up. It was a real stretch for her to believe us but, perhaps, one of the early ways we built trust. *We promise we will see you after your nap. We will keep you safe.* Her vigilance would have to be aborted in favour of letting go. This was a big ask for a child who coped with early adoption trauma with vigilance and her need to be in control. It made sense, then, that early on she didn't let us hold her, except on her terms.

After they were securely asleep we turned the car around, for if we turned around before Franny was asleep, she would take it as a sign of encouragement and force herself awake. Also, she would then know that either we abandoned our trip to Sleepy Hollow or no such place existed. Occasionally I would pull in to a quiet spot, a park or a dirt road with a lake view, and close my eyes too. Despite my exhaustion, I never managed to sleep in the car. Still, a short rest in a reclined car seat was much better than crying babies.

However, I felt more than a pang of guilt combusting fossil fuels for this endeavour. I would hope I didn't run into anyone, particularly when I turned around at Kokanee Creek Provincial Park. More than once, I babbled on to people who weren't judging me, explaining what I was doing and why. I didn't tell many people that I did this on a frequent basis, least of all my environmental-consultant friends. This was a sure sign I was a full-fledged Kootenay resident, for I wouldn't have given it a second thought in Toronto. I know that it was not selfish, that my own sanity depended upon it and that I did not want to be personally responsible for putting Nelson on the map as a town where a deranged adoptive lesbian mom was charged with infanticide.

Sometimes we ended up at Six Mile, on a few occasions at Twelve Mile. Yes, those demarcations are what they sound like, six miles from town and so on, unoriginal but straightforward. There are actually towns in BC called 100 Mile House and 150 Mile House, so named during the gold rush for their distances from Lillooet on the Old Cariboo Road. Distance is paramount in a vast landscape with miles of no habitation, people mere punctuations in the topography.

I'd drive home, sleepy myself, park and quietly open the back doors of our Subaru. Removing the twins' car seat restraints was an art form, as was gently getting one's hands around the babies' backs and lifting them up without their heads flopping or their torsos slipping down to an ungainly angle between one's hands. I'd long ago given up avoiding being smeared with soggy Nutri-Grain bars from the twins' flaccid fists or faces. They were usually half draped with their pint-sized travel blankets sweetly made by a friend of a friend who'd met them only once: Theo's with navy fleece on one side and cotton yellow bears and tents on the other, Franny's with purple fleece and a print of white, yellow and purple flowers. I'd reposition the blankets loosely over their heads to shade them from any sun and insulate them from neighbourhood noise.

When transferring the twins one at a time to their cribs, I was grateful they were small and light for their age. This was a delicate operation, one that could so easily be thwarted by an unaware neighbour starting up a lawn mower or shouting hello, by a belligerent crow cawing its possessiveness over our cherry tree. We don't have a garage, attached or otherwise. Even posh Victorian-era houses simply don't. It is likely that our house plans were originally purchased from the Sears Roebuck catalogue at the turn of the nineteenth century. The original house would have closely resembled my grandmother's two-up, two-down in northern England, complete with a coal fire in the front room, the indoor plumbing, lake view and later a large kitchen addition notwithstanding.

We also have an alley parking spot above our garden. Everything is on a slope or terraced in this mountainside town. I'd walk down two different sets of stairs, along our uneven stepping stones in our backyard, and open the French door into the kitchen. Here I'd pause to slip off the twins' shoes or boots and sometimes my own if I felt lucky, for this was always a risky move balancing on one foot with a toddler in one's arms. I'd walk through the house, softly treading on the fir floors, whose gaps were almost as wide as the boards. There was the real danger of puncturing bare feet with a sliver. Our kids later called them "splinter floors," in fact, and knew how to extract their own slivers from three years old onward. I would creep up the old creaky steps into their small room, where I'd lift them each over the side of the crib, typically with their jackets and sometimes snow pants still on. This was always dangerous because they'd wake up too hot, but the alternative was unthinkable.

In the early days, I'd worry myself sick before I returned to the car to retrieve twin number two. I'd wonder how I'd live with myself or how to defend myself if anything happened to the one left behind. I'd imagine the abandoned one confronting us in therapy years later: *I always knew I was not the favourite because you left me in the car.* Which twin stayed in the car was determined by a few factors: which one would be more likely to remain asleep, who had been soundly asleep the longest and could more likely withstand the upheaval at that time.

Nothing bad ever happened and a few months in, we stopped worrying so much about kidnappers or a frightening sound that would startle them awake. Our biggest worry was that the one remaining in the car would wake up and find themselves abandoned, reinforcing the deep-seated feeling that they were alone in this world, despite all our attempts at attachment. We eventually started to trust they'd be okay for the three minutes it would take us to return and no longer felt the need to sprint back to the car. It was on one of these days that I awoke from a nap, feeling disturbed. "Amy, I had such a weird dream. I was clearing a playground of land mines. It was a playground we frequented and my job was to complete this before Theo and Franny could safely play."

"Oh God, that sounds awful."

"Yeah, I felt such a sense of doom. What if I missed just one cluster bomb and the kids thought it was a toy? They would die or get a leg blown off."

"No pressure," said Amy.

We relaxed a little, but not much, which may well be how we still approach parenting. Not as relaxed as we would like, worrying about things over which we have no control in the middle of the night, such as how adoption trauma will impact them in adolescence and, after we get through that, in adulthood. The day-to-day stuff we are pretty chill about. We found that out when our city friends went to the playground with us and were horrified that we would picnic fifty metres away with our backs turned while our eight-year-olds played on the climbing equipment. "Aren't you worried about them falling or weirdos taking them?"

"No. We hadn't even thought of it." Amy and I looked at each other and shrugged.

Danger or not, by some kind of miracle, the majority of the time they wouldn't wake up during the nap transfer. Sometimes I would so crave quiet time that I would read or write during their nap, but most often I flopped down, exhausted, for a nap too. Sometimes one would awake on the transfer and the whole plan would evaporate as tears of exhaustion streamed down my cheeks. Sometimes I'd get them into bed and one would wake up and I'd have to evacuate the awake one as quickly as a marine would extract a person down in a military operation. Having one up had the same outcome as having both up: no nap for the adults, though sometimes it was slightly easier having one rather than two to entertain. So much depended upon the nap: our sanity, for instance.

Fortunately, they slept in the same room until they were eight years old. We put an addition on our over-hundred-year-old home, making it a three-bedroom instead of a two-bedroom. They'd still have sleepovers with each other but their need to differentiate won out over bonding time. Besides, Franny would keep the light on or talk too long and keep Theo up so she could put off the inevitable. She frequently charms my wife into long conversations at bedtime until I, the bad guy, shut it down. Otherwise she is grumpy the next day, plus we need a few minutes of couple time, which too often translates into scheduling and other mundane tasks. But that is another story and one that won't be unfamiliar to any other parents.

Even now, as a preteen, Franny resists falling asleep and still has amazing staying power for wakefulness. These days she bends herself in half while lying down and puts her legs over her head. Or she climbs her ever-lankier legs up along a wall while lying on the floor. They say this position, where blood flows to the head, can help you stay awake when sleepy. Let's call it an effective substitute for yawning. We have a rule that she can't go upside down after dinner.

Once in a while they still both fall asleep driving home from a day of skiing or a soccer tournament. When she lets herself fall asleep, our tough, persistent Franny does not look as if she feels as betrayed but there is a remnant of that alarmed look in her eyes. We still tell her it's okay, that we'll be here when she wakes. She laughs but also takes comfort in us knowing this about her, even though she and Theo speak of Sleepy Hollow both as a betrayal and with a wink and a nod. "You told us it was a place, Mom!"

SITTING DUCKS

A few months into our parenting adventures, when we were exhausted and stretched to our capacity, the manager of adoption services from the Ministry of Children and Family Development called us. "I am sorry to have to tell you this, but your children's birth mother has some identifying information about you that she is not supposed to have."

"How do you know this? How did she get it?"

"One of my staff, a social worker, was meeting with the birth mom and she left the room to photocopy something. Unfortunately, she left a document in the meeting room. She was only gone a minute but when she returned it was missing." I couldn't believe what I was hearing. I held my breath. "When the birth mother denied taking the missing document, my staff had no choice but to report it."

"Why was the information left in the room?" I asked.

"Yes, that was a mistake. The social worker feels terrible. She wants to call you to apologize," the manager said.

"That's fine but what does this mean for us? Will the birth mother show up at our door?" I asked.

"It is very unlikely. I have checked with the adoption social worker, Maryann, who knows the birth mom better. She says the birth mom does not have the resources or likely the inclination to come to your house. She says she's not dangerous."

They reported the breach and the birth mom's name to the RCMP, in the unlikely event she showed up. To say that we were in shock is an understatement. We were still on probation; the adoption hadn't been finalized. Our adoption agreement with the birth mother was semi-open, meaning we were expected to write letters and send pictures to her that did not use last names or give away any details about where we lived. She agreed to do the same. Nothing had changed with the birth mom since we signed the semi-openness agreement in terms of it being okay for our children to now have direct contact, so the agreement needed to stand. The Adoption Exchange, a third party, would remove any identifying information, repackage letters in their own envelopes and send them on so the birth mother wouldn't have our address. While adoption social workers make every effort for adoptions to be open, with contact between birth families and adoptive families, in our particular case the ministry social workers recommended this limited connection because they believed it was in the best interest of our children.

The social worker who breached our confidentiality called. There were tears all around as she expressed her profound regret and we expressed our fears.

Document in hand, the birth mother now knew that a same-sex couple had adopted the twins, not to mention where we lived. We were concerned that this would result in her contesting the adoption, given that it was never her choice. The ministry had taken her children at birth because of concerns and a prior history of having her other children removed from her care. We also knew she had religious relatives and worried that they might revisit the possibility of adopting the kids within their family, as had been done with our children's four half-siblings and one full sibling. The social worker who knew the birth mother best told us that this was an unlikely scenario, that the birth mother was not likely functional enough to mount an appeal. She reiterated that the birth mom likely didn't have the resources to trek to our doorstep now that she knew our address. Still, Amy and I felt very much like we were sitting ducks. While I had empathy for the birth mom's profound loss, I also had my mama-bear instincts. We already lived with the vigilance that is required when you suddenly have two toddlers exploring and regularly breaching what you thought of as your childproofing, and now this confidentiality breach made us hypervigilant.

Our high cortisol levels were also a result of an adoption that hadn't yet been finalized and hence could still be undone, as well as having twins who were at times inconsolable due to grief piled upon grief and loss upon loss. This loss was mostly related to leaving their foster parents, their only caregivers, who had loved them and cared for them since they left the hospital shortly after birth. They also experienced non-verbal loss, from nine months in their birth mother's womb, knowing her heartbeat and then knowing her smell when they were born.

Amy and I quietly freaked out every time there was a knock at our door or we could hear voices nearby. Our friends knew the situation so they would always call ahead and never arrive unannounced at our doorstep. We also found ourselves having to inform a wider circle of caregivers and neighbours. It was uncomfortable yet necessary. Nobody was allowed to take, let alone post, photos of our kids anywhere. We found our barely used house key (we live in Nelson, after all) and locked our doors when we were out during the day and even when we were inside. We were grateful we had a large dog. We were on the lookout for Indian women when we were out in public, which tells you what you need to know about the demographics of our town at the time.

I tried not to think about it but what-ifs crept in, usually in the middle of the night. What if she contests? What if she shows up on our doorstep? We had heard too many heartbreaking stories of adoptive parents having babies taken back because birth families changed their minds, especially fuelled by birth families who learn that "their" baby is going to a same-sex couple. Granted, this usually happened within the two-week period immediately after a birth, when the birth parents choose to place their child for adoption. But we were always cautioned that despite the slim chances, adoptions could be contested any time during the probation period of nine months. After seven months of bonding with the twins and having their tiny fingers wrapped completely around our hearts, it was inconceivable that we could lose them.

The ever-present threat of homophobia reared its ugly head. I was on alert. We collaborated on developing a safety plan with the ministry. This plan required us to notify the RCMP if the birth mom contacted us in any way, at which point the ministry's legal counsel would seek a protective intervention order. We were told to plan for the worst, which consisted of imagining that the birth mother would show up and try to take the twins or in any way scare them or compromise their safety. It was unlikely to happen. Nevertheless it was our worst fear. This situation was in part why we decided to take an extended beach vacation that first year of being a family. It helped that we had the freedom of being on parental leave. Nobody would find us at my in-laws' condo in southwest Florida.

It is not straightforward to travel internationally with children who are formally still in the guardianship of the Province of British Columbia. As a same-sex white couple with brown babies, we knew we were likely to be asked for identification when travelling. Because we didn't have access to the twins' birth certificates, they had no identification with which to cross the border. Without the birth certificates, we also could not apply to add the children to our passports. New birth certificates are issued when the adoption is formally complete. (Does this make our children "born again"?) The original birth certificates are sealed. Children may see their originals when they are adults with the birth parents' consent. It is one of the many ways that adoptive kids are cut off from their origin stories. This sits uneasily with me, yet I understand the why behind it, the need to protect kids. Adoptive families are not allowed to know their children's full names or those of their birth parents for confidentiality reasons, except in some open adoption situations.

We got letters of permission from the ministry, which was the official guardian. US customs could not guarantee our admittance to their country with these letters, even though we faxed them to our closest border crossing. We took a chance anyway and bought plane tickets from Spokane, Washington, a three-hour drive and our nearest major airport. The female customs officer at our minuscule border crossing in the middle of the mountains, having seen us multiple times as a childless couple, even congratulated us on adopting the kids. Not at all what we expected at the US border.

On the flights from Spokane to Florida, we had to get used to attention, both negative and positive. The flight attendants were kind and well meaning with their "Where are your kids from?" (Canada) and "What is their first language?" (English … but for now "toddler babble"). There was no more anonymous travel where those who wanted to could see us as two friends on a trip. We were clearly a family, two moms and two active toddlers. We didn't have surplus energy for staring strangers who behaved as if they had never seen a lesbian couple before, when our focus was just to contain the twins in our row of seats. It was a whole other level of coming out that stretched us outside the progressive bubble of Nelson.

It was worth it. We left the boots and snow pants behind and happily walked along the beach, smelling the hot salt air while the toddlers pointed excitedly at the pelicans that swooped down into the Gulf of Mexico for their suppers each evening. We enjoyed the tamer pastime of bobbing with the toddlers in the pool at the condo complex even if it was almost impossible to relax in the hot tub as the sun set. Not having to bundle up twin toddlers in order to go out for a walk was a revelation and a delight. It more than made up for feeling like fish out of water in southwest Florida.

It was during our Florida visit that we received an email from the ministry. After the confidentiality breach, and all the follow-up letters of apology and explanations of how they would change their procedures to ensure it wouldn't happen again to anyone else, I opened it with trepidation. *Congrat-ulations, your adoption order has been granted by the Supreme Court of British Columbia. You are the official guardians of Frances and Theodore.* I had to read it twice to believe it. My eyes danced over these happy words. It was exactly nine months to the day since we had brought them home, just as our social worker had said we could expect if all went smoothly. We cried and danced around the condo, each of us with an oblivious toddler in our arms. "We are a forever family!" we exclaimed.

We celebrated with a trip to an old-school Dairy Queen, where we sat outside on faded red plastic seats and mopped up liquefied soft serve from our toddlers' chins and arms as traffic whizzed by on the adjacent eight-lane highway. Our worries melted away too, albeit not as quickly as the ice cream in the South Florida sun. It was made sweeter by the irony that we were celebrating in one of only two states that banned same-sex couples from adopting children.

We got them both vanilla cones because it was easier to mop up from toddler hands than chocolate. We discovered Theo's love of chocolate-dipped cones only later on; what he didn't know didn't hurt him. His lip-smacking feedback was enough to convince us we nailed it. And this is how parenting works: you try something, it works, you go with it until proven otherwise. It was the happiest ice cream I've ever eaten and though my epicurean self would much rather have had local, organic, hand-churned hippie ice cream while sitting in the woods, there is still a special place in my heart for soft serve, chocolate dipped or not, along the interstate.

A Journey with Dad

In October 2003, my father flew from Toronto to Kelowna, where I picked him up and we drove the windy road through the Monashees from Vernon to Nakusp, then to my off-grid cabin in the Slocan Valley. The drive is mountainous, most of the slopes densely covered in needled trees, with occasional dramatic views of Upper Arrow Lake. The so-called lake is not a lake at all, but a reservoir. This fact only increased my father's curiosity about harnessing the wild for electrical power. By the time we arrived, we needed a flashlight to walk the five-hundred-metre footpath through the pitch-black forest past the outhouse to my one-room cabin. The two-burner cooktop perched upon the wooden cupboards, fashioned from the surrounding fir trees, the gas lamps, the small table where I wrote poems and love letters to Amy, the little wood stove and the double bed were all there was to it. I felt a mixture of pride and embarrassment showing him around. "This is it, where I've stayed for two months."

"Hmm, it is spartan. Your mother wouldn't like it."

"No. But it's been a great retreat for me. Hauling firewood in exchange for rent feels good and is a nice break from writing. The owner raised her three children in the cabin for a few years."

"What a childhood they must have had running in the woods, no TV. Amazing." My father helped me carry my few possessions, books and journals, a box of food and a suitcase of clothing, down to the car the next morning. I turned back and said goodbye to the empty cabin, one that a trapper could have felt at home in last century. Apartment hunting in downtown Toronto, my first order of business upon return from my seven-month sabbatical, felt like a million miles away. We spent a few days in Nelson saying goodbye to my newfound community, seven months of nourishing myself culminating in a farewell party generously hosted by friends. I showed him my life as I'd lived it for the past seven months. He seemed amazed that people carve out such interesting, unconventional lives: my vegetarian organic food catering friend, my friend who teaches self-defence to women in India, my friend who does creative metalwork—all livelihoods he hadn't thought existed. Not to mention all my friends in forestry and environmental work, which are not prevalent occupations in southern Ontario. When we departed, sated with hugs and poems, he said, "You've made quite a life for yourself. This is an amazing place."

"Yeah, I always knew I'd love living and backpacking in the mountains after visiting Nelson. But I'm surprised by the friends and sense of community I feel here. Like we are all connected."

"You sound like you are New Age."

"I do feel like we are all connected and that there is something bigger than us."

"Like what, God?"

"Not exactly," I explained. "I felt it in anatomy class the first time we saw the cadavers. Like our human system was too complex to be random." I still have a clear memory of the cadavers. They got wrapped in formaldehyde-soaked canvas at the end of each class. Each cadaver was sawn in half longitudinally, no skin except the retracted bit on the skull. I became accustomed to but was never without wonder at mapping arteries until they became capillaries, as David Thompson mapped our rivered part of the world. The intricacies and beautiful design of body systems, the fan of gluteal muscle, all the wondrous angles it could extend and abduct the leg, for walking up mountains, for playing football, for sex. "Anatomy class made me believe both more and less in God. More, because it is difficult to imagine a system so well designed without a creator," I offered.

"Evolution. It's evolution," my father said.

"Evolution is beyond our scope to fully know and it took wild acts of imagination to come up with the theory. Evolution is being able to imagine into being a metropolis and then a whole world, while only ever living in a hamlet. The evolutionary pace of change is so subtle it is beyond fathoming," I opined.

My father smiled. "Thanks to Darwin." After he retired, my father, an atheist, took a mini-medical school course at the Queen's University School of Medicine. His friends, who had no such aspirations, teased him for being a mini-doctor. I imagine he saw arterial systems as the electrical systems he knew so well. He was shunted toward an electrical apprenticeship, told he'd be a good electrician because he worked the lights at a school play and because, as a working-class male in England, a technical trade was the opportunity available to him. His later thirst for Isaac Asimov and Stephen Hawking, for flight simulators and for medicine made it apparent he would have gone on to bigger things had he not been constrained by the class system in Britain.

"You sound like you believe in intelligent design," my father said.

"What does Christopher Hitchens say about that?" I asked.

"He debunks creationists," said my dad.

"I don't believe in creationism. I am a scientist. I just have this feeling of something larger than me. I know I'm not very articulate about it."

The truth is I'm cozied up to atheism with a small side of *We are all connected*. I enjoyed this banter immensely and my sense was that my father did too.

On the drive through the BC interior, he talked about the formidable landscape more than once. "This terrain is amazing. How they put power lines through here is beyond me. And the dams, it's hard to conceive of that much power. I would have loved to work here."

"I thought you applied to BC Hydro."

"No, I never did. I wanted to but your mother didn't want to move again." My mother was already pushed to her westerly limit, it seems, with the move from England to Ontario.

"Tell me about your time in Cyprus." I wanted to hear my dad's stories about when he felt free.

"I was on a mountain rescue team stationed in Cyprus, keeping the peace between the Greeks and the Turks. This was in the Royal Air Force in the days of mandatory service."

"Did you have to rescue anyone?"

"Mostly each other from drinking too much. It was pretty quiet. We got to hike and practise rescues."

"What about when you worked on ships? Wasn't that your military service?" I wasn't used to having this time with my dad to ask about his life before he had a family.

"No, it was the British merchant marine. I was the electrician on board the ship. An officer. I travelled everywhere, the Mediterranean, Suez Canal, the Gulf of Oman."

"What about the Himalayas?" I pronounced it like Sir Edmund Hillary would have, *Him-ALL-yas*. Not *Him-a-LAY-as* like the rest of us pronounced it, a running family joke and ongoing irritant to my mother.

"No, not the *Him-ALL-yas*," he said with a glimmer in his eye.

"Did you like it?"

"I loved it. I tried to return to the merchant marine after I met your mother but she refused to live like that."

"I guess she didn't want to be away from you." I swallowed hard and hesitated, then asked, "Do you regret your decisions?"

"It would have been fun, but I like living in Canada and I wouldn't have had a family. So, it worked out."

"Glad to hear," I said.

I know from my mother that he gave her an ultimatum when it seemed impossible to get ahead in northern England. It was 1970 and the mills were shutting down in Great Britain. The *Great* was continuing its long slip through the open hands of Britain. He told my mom they would either emigrate from northern England to Canada or he was returning to the merchant marine.

"That takes a lot of courage. Moving to a new continent with fifty dollars in your pocket, a young wife and young child. No friends," I said.

My father shrugged. "It worked out fine. Besides, it was a choice. It wasn't like I was a child shipped away from his parents during the war. Like the children in London," my father said.

"I guess, but I still think it takes courage to do what you did. I am very grateful that you chose Canada. I don't think I would have as good a life. I don't think I would have had the opportunity to go to university." I wanted to spell it out; my dad was the epitome of the understated English of that generation who lived through bombing raids and losing their dads to war, through either death or shell shock. As a six-year-old, he looked after his sister while his father was losing his mind and spirit as a medic in northern Africa and my grandmother was working long shifts in the munitions factory.

Our drive back to Ontario was the last hurrah of my adventure before I returned to my Toronto life and my dad returned to Kingston and my mother, who was nervous without him. We camped across the prairies after escaping the grey shroud of the Rockies in late October. In Brooks, Alberta, the air is ripe with smells from the abattoir—Canada's largest beef processing and packing plant. My father was a vegetarian and I was ready to return to this diet after the stench and the thought of four thousand beef cattle a day being slaughtered. We decamped early, in time to watch the red hue of sunrise, made tea on the one-burner stove and got egg sandwiches without bacon on the road. I had a smattering of regret that my father and I had not camped together other than this, as he clearly loved it.

For much of the drive across the prairies he stared in wonder at all the space with so few people. We had anticipated that the Rockies would be the highlight of this trip but in late October they were all but invisible. The fog and rain set in and we could barely tell we were in the mountains, except for listening to my Ford Focus wagon labour up passes and seeing scatterings of fresh snow patches. It was the prairie sky that took our breath away, the sunrise over golden fields as we listened to Keith Jarrett's improvised piano music.

As our trip's end came near, I was torn between wanting to find out more about my father's life and the anticipation of seeing the woman I had not seen for six months and fell in love with through letters. Amy had declared us officially dating since Labour Day weekend, when for twenty-four hours she was a licensed marriage official in order to officiate at her friend's wedding in New England. As my father and I drove south on progressively larger highways toward the Greater Toronto Area, the anticipation expanded until I could barely think of anything else. I was smitten, listening to a CD that Amy had made and sent me for the drive across the country. At the end of the drive, I ended up at her third-storey flat in Cabbagetown, my dad in tow. He graciously waited outside while I went in and had the biggest hello kiss of my life. We all went out for a beer and though we offered my dad a place to stay, he opted to get on a night bus back to Kingston, remarking, "It's been a long time since I've felt that way about someone." He was smirking as he said this and embarked. I was elated that my father had met her, that I was at the beginning of this journey with my future wife and at the end of the greatest adventure I'd ever had up to that point.

My father loved our cross-country adventure, as I came to learn, after I talked to my mother and his friends. I regret not taking him through the Rockies again in better weather and perhaps in the comfort of an RV, but this was limited by my mother's anxiety around road trips. Every mountain would elicit a sharp sucking in of breath through her teeth as she wondered what danger lurked at each pass and curve in the road. The lower back pain that sitting in a vehicle seemed to cause didn't endear long drives to her either. Instead my father would have to settle for flying to Nelson and driving up the Kootenay River, looking at the dams and marvelling at the Selkirk Mountains on subsequent trips.

Aging parents and indeed the death of a parent render many past mistakes benign. My last words to my father, and his to me, were "I love you." That I'm able to give my children the gift of seeing them and imparting some emotional intelligence is in no small part a result of what my parents gave me. I couldn't expect them to be providing beauty when they were busy providing a foundation in this country. That I needed beauty was beside the point. It was mine to figure out. And besides, my father bought a used book of poems, Lawrence Ferlinghetti's *A Coney Island of the Mind*, with his first bit of pocket money after he moved to Canada, once the furniture necessities had been bought. He gave me permission to go searching.

At my father's celebration of life in a condo party room in my parents' building, I stood up and said a few words:

> My father built an ultra-lightweight airplane when I was ten or so. He worked on it every night, when he wasn't working shifts or overtime. As he welded it together, his aluminum frame started to look like a cockpit for one person. I don't know where he got the design, but *Popular Mechanics* magazines were always piled in his workshop. Unfortunately for him, he built the aircraft in the basement and had no way to get it out. It sat there for years, a point of ridicule for his friends and family. That he built it at all was admirable. He never flew on his own steam but he went on to other dreams. He built his own electric bikes long before they became popular or even commercially available. This was in order to overcome cycling limitations due to an unheard of third knee replacement on the same knee. I feel as if I carry his determination and intellectual curiosity forward. I got to live out that curiosity more fully, having had the privilege of a university education. I feel forever grateful to my father for encouraging it in me and for immigrating to Canada, where there was more opportunity to transcend class.

Sometimes when I'm alone I wander the house and look at the picture of my dad that adorns our mantle. His warm smile—a selfie he took a couple of years before he died, on what would be their last trip to England together—melts me and I smile back. Even his nose, scarred and misshapen from a motorbike accident in his twenties, is familiar rather than ugly to me. I talk to him infrequently and briefly. "Hi, Dad. I miss you. I miss talking to you about everyday and worldly things."

Early Kid Days

We were bleary-eyed mothers. Our friends dropped off meals and clothes. We went from gourmet dinners to finishing the kids' leftover, bland, slobbery fish soup while walking around in a sleep-deprived fog. We hunkered in and held them a lot those first months. The first year was a blur. The irony that our sexual orientation was an obstacle in adoption and the post-adoptive reality of life with twin toddlers was not lost on us. Never had I felt less like a lesbian in all my life. Too tired for sex, too frazzled to finish any conversations with friends about what rights were being won or lost in the world. We would remark that our lesbian "membership cards" would be revoked any day. It was a major shift in our respective identities to be mothers first: tectonic plates shifting. When I came out it was a more gradual shift in plates, the quiet realization of a zing through my body as I not only noticed a woman who was attractive in a general sense, but was attracted to her. The visceral power ensured I could not deny it, though I tried. The shift into motherhood was more like an eight on the Richter scale. The earth moved after living on the assumption it was solid. Mothering careening twin toddlers was a seismic shift. I'm not sure I knew my name those first few months. Perhaps it was just that my name didn't matter. My name was Mom.

Going for a walk was carefully considered and best done with equal numbers of adults and children. That is why my partner and I often walked together, but when Amy returned to her business of making movies and running film camp later that first year, I was on my own with the kids. Sometimes a generous friend came along to help with the two kids, who wanted to escape the double stroller, and our golden retriever, who would take any opportunity to run off in search of garbage.

One day Franny and Theo, needing to move their bodies, liberated themselves from their stroller and ran off in different directions, Franny down to the main street of town and Theo up the hill away from town. Franny was upset because I had said no to going to the shops and Theo was upset because his sister was. "Franny, sweetie, come back," I said to the back of her toddler form as she ran downhill toward our main street. "Theo, let's go see the pond. Come here, sweetie," I urged to the back of him as he lumbered uphill away from the main street.

Frozen in an impossible triage-decision moment, I heard, "How can I help? Which one should I run after?" It was a neighbour I barely knew who, true to her occupation as a magician, appeared out of nowhere.

"If you can grab Theo up there, that would help." Theo continued his lumbering walk-run away from us while crying.

I ran downhill toward Franny. "Come here, baby."

"Uuuunnnnnnnnhhhh!" she screamed. I was gaining on her, just barely.

"Franny, please stop. You can't go by yourself."

When I caught up to her she screeched, "Nooooo!" Her squid-like limbs were elusive as I tried to pick her up.

I heard Theo up the hill in the distance. He was crying and freaked out that a stranger was walking him back to me, though she had the good sense not to pick him up, and by then he wanted me. "Wow, I don't know what I would have done without your help. Thank you so much," I said.

"I'm glad I was walking by. You've got your hands full."

"Yeah, we call them the turbo twins."

❦

After the first few months of being home with them and introducing them to only our closest friends, friends whom we banked on being around for a while, we ventured to a party hosted by one of these couples. Unfinished sentences, unfinished burgers and a terraced lawn with rock walls punctuated our experience. Our kids were filthy from the combination of sticking their hands in hummus and guacamole and falling on the ground—dip, dirt and weave. At that party, a friend of a friend asked which one of us was the mother. The rest of the guests stopped their conversations, paused taking bites of their burgers. Most of them recognized that we both were and they stared in wonderment at how we'd handle this.

My ever-gracious partner said, "We both are." We moved on. I didn't appreciate having to deal with this question when I had very little capacity to deal with anything other than keeping two toddlers safe, with all that mobility and no sense. We took turns but one parent could simply not run after two speedy, curious little ones in that psychic and physical terrain. As neither of us could socialize with the adults, we gave up after a short time and went home. This was our life now.

Our own yard is full of rock walls. I would often leave the French doors open as I walked through into our kitchen so the kids could stay outside on the deck. One day, when the kids were four years old, as I quickly prepared a snack for them, their happy noises turned to silence. Too quiet is never a good thing. I ventured outside to see my daughter standing underneath my son, propping him up while he attempted to climb the rock wall. "You can do it, Theo," she said.

"No, stop. He can't and you shouldn't be underneath him. Not safe," I said.

"I want to climb. Safe," Theo pronounced.

"Good teamwork, you guys. But I don't want your head bouncing off rocks all the way down our terraced garden," I tried to explain.

"I keep my brother safe," Franny declared.

"Let's use your skills somewhere else. Maybe building blocks?" I was saved by snack time.

In order to attach, we felt we needed to be the primary caregivers for our kids. It worked out well, not only because we were fortunate enough to be able to stay home for more than three years between us, but also because we both spelled each other off so we knew what an exhausting, difficult job it was to be home with twins. We knew what the other meant when one of us said we cried at nap time because one of the kids didn't sleep and woke the other and then that was it, no break or rest time. I remember looking at the clock in disbelief that it was only 9:00 a.m. sometimes. At a particularly low time, I actually emailed a group of friends asking for help however they could provide it, taking the kids for an hour, taking our dog for a walk, making us some food. It wasn't like me to ask; in fact, I really was desperate. It surprised Amy. "You emailed our friends asking for help?"

"I'm just feeling like I can't do it all anymore. I know I should have told you first. It was hard for me to ask, and I just did it in a wits'-end kind of moment." Some friends stepped up; many were surprised that I would ask. I guess I appear competent. I also don't easily show vulnerability.

Overwhelmed as I was, why was it, then, that I went all *Julie & Julia* and decided to cook my way through a cookbook, and a complicated one at that?

I was under some illusion that I needed something tangible to accomplish. As if keeping twins fed, in dry diapers and safe at two years old wasn't enough. Supporting our children to attach instead of supporting injured workers in their seismic shifts into different occupations after serious injury, and writing poems in a quiet living room before work, was my new reality. Settling into motherhood was a shift from intellectual to mundane and emotional. I was seriously worried I'd forget how to write but I couldn't generate poems, which require deep contemplation and quiet. Sleep deprivation and constant noise ensured that couldn't happen. Instead, I cooked my way through Shelley Adams's *Whitewater Cooks with Friends*, her second publication in an enormously popular series of cookbooks following her very successful stint as ski-hill owner and head chef of the lodge restaurant, Fresh Tracks Cafe. In true Nelson fashion, our ski-hill restaurant has the best food I've ever eaten on the side of a snowy mountain. Here is an excerpt from my cooking blog at that time:

> Remember those iceberg lettuce/anaemic salads from childhood. Well, from my childhood. Not just at my house but at every restaurant in rural Ontario. You know the ones, they had "Eye-talian" dressing and a shave of carrot, sometimes a thin slice of pink tomato and nary a nutrient. Thankfully house salads have come a long way. I think it's a testament to our "cultural mosaic" that house salads have evolved to include seeds and Mediterranean cheese. I make this salad frequently, a true house salad. It's got all the basics: lettuce, some grated root vegetable (beet), some feta, some tomatoes and some seeds. It's a nice touch with the fresh dill.
>
> My twins (2 yrs old) love helping. One of the jobs they can be successful at is tearing lettuce. My son, who seems to be more detail oriented, carefully tears one lettuce leaf into uniform miniature bite size pieces. My speed-queen daughter tears each leaf in two large pieces if you're lucky. Her goal is to get through her stack of lettuce at luge-like speed (sorry, it's the Olympics as I write this). She's usually finished her pile before her brother is finished tearing his first piece. We don't need to buy mixed greens anymore; the twins do the work of lettuce preparation.
>
> Eating your greens has never been so easy. Bon appétit.

Making any food dish, even something as simple as a salad, was always done on edge. One step from out of control. A girl who's finished her lettuce prep climbs on the counter needing something else to do. The boy still tearing his lettuce but wanting to be on the counter too, and then the ever-present fall hazard. I couldn't let them make vinaigrette. So the salad gets abandoned for a few hours and we move to the playroom. It was often like this, daylong prep, always triaging, pre-empting or managing a tantrum or a careening toddler looking for something shiny and fun, not unlike a magpie.

Although exhausted, I would sometimes cook while the kids napped, so desperate was I for creativity and a semblance of my previous life. And it had been swallowed up in the profound shift in our lives. Making a dressing, composing torn lettuce and roasting seeds were all orders of magnitude more difficult than they were pre-kids.

WE HAVE TWO MOMMIES

At home in the small, progressive city we live in, we are easy to spot coming down the street—two moms with twins of colour. Some days, it feels like everyone knows us or knows of us. I feel our differences most acutely when travelling to Bible belts: the Okanagan or the US Midwest. Pre-kids we only caught the eye of other lesbian couples when travelling. We are so clearly a unit now, kids yelling "Look, Mama! Look, Mom!" We get stared at. Sometimes it's amusing but mostly it's tiring. We answer questions such as "What do they call each of you?" and "Do you have male role models?" My personal favourite happened in an elevator in Florida. An older woman in creased white slacks, a floral blouse and matching purse—dare I say a lady who does lunch and likely some philanthropy on the side—asked, "Which one of you is the mom?"

In unison, Amy and I said, "We both are." She turned her taut face away from us and urgently pushed the elevator buttons, trying to escape, as if we were contagious. We broke out into full-on guffaws when she walked off the elevator. "Holy fuck, did that just happen?" I asked.

At home in Nelson, at four years old, Franny came home from daycare and said, "My friend at school says that boys can only marry girls. She said girls can't marry girls and boys can't marry boys."

I looked at her and said, "Well, I'm a girl and I'm married to Mama, who is also a girl, so girls can definitely marry girls and boys can marry boys too."

That night we pulled out our now well-worn copy of *And Tango Makes Three*. It is a non-fiction children's book about two male penguins at the New York City zoo who are partners and try to hatch an egg-shaped rock. The zookeeper gives them an untended egg, which they care for until it hatches. Then they become a family with their female offspring, Tango. Homosexuality can hardly be cast as a disease or a lifestyle choice under this circumstance, and the book lacks any moral condemnation for the penguins. At the time, it was the most banned book in North America. Franny marched back to daycare the next day and found her friend right away. "You are wrong! Girls can marry girls and boys can marry boys too."

I stood there watching, waiting. The little girl looked at me, confused. I shrugged and said, "I'm a girl and I'm married to another girl."

The friend seemed satisfied and said, "Okay. Do you want to play with the blocks?" Off they went.

Daycare was just a warm-up for taking our space in the world. We were one of two lesbian-parent families in our children's kindergarten class. We were not pioneers. We met with each of the two kindergarten teachers at our school so we could make an informed request about who we felt would be the best match. We were immediately put at ease by one of the teachers, who let us know that she not only was adopted but also had seen my partner's documentary, *Conceiving Family*, about same-sex couples adopting, including our story. Whew. No explanation needed.

It seemed like some sort of cruel joke that Franny picked the Mormon kid to be her best friend in kindergarten. "Lydia can only marry a boy," she announced after school one day. "Lydia's mom told her she had to marry a boy." I told Franny she could marry whomever she wants and so could Lydia. This was an interesting twist on the "Girls can only marry boys," a subtle shift. Now Lydia was being told she could only marry a boy instead of being told that girls can only marry boys. This is the subtle shift that happens when same-sex marriages are legalized. In Canada, it is simply a fact that it is legal. Our relationships are legitimized as a result. The Mormons have to change their messaging to "Our children have to marry the opposite sex."

The kindergarten teacher had overheard this conversation between Franny and Lydia and had mentioned it to us. When I asked her how she responded, she said she didn't say anything, just listened. "If this comes up again, you need to teach what is the law, that yes, men can marry men and women can marry women," I said. "Whatever Lydia's parents are teaching her is not the law and is in fact a fringe belief." The open-hearted teacher reluctantly agreed that if it came up she would address it, though she was visibly uncomfortable at the thought of inadvertently offending another family's beliefs. *Good luck, Lydia*, I thought. *Good luck, mom of Lydia*, if Lydia falls in love with a woman. But maybe it'll be better by then. Maybe.

Although we see glimpses of our kids trying to conform, which seems age appropriate, we have no worries that our kids won't rise to the challenges with the same panache my daughter showed at daycare or that my son models for his classmates by playing house with a mom and a mama. On the other hand, we have had more than a handful of children come over to us at school pickup or drop-off and say, "Aw, Franny and Theo are lucky because they have two moms." When I ask why they are lucky, I've heard "My dad is strict" or "My mom is nicer" or "My dad works away." It was a sweet irony when Theo brought home his kindergarten picture holding up a sign of what he wanted to be when he grows up and it said simply "Dad."

We are loosely connected to the adoptive families network in our region. It feels important for our kids to see and interact with other adoptive children and, at times, it has been important for us to connect with other parents as well. On our first adoptive families camping weekend, in which there were many white parents and even more brown kids, we felt both a sense of belonging and that we stood out because we were the only queer parents. Our kids also stood out as two of the few adoptive kids with Indian heritage. We were told by social workers that typically Indian-heritage families absorb kids who need adopting within extended families, even more than in other cultures. I am uncertain if this extends to other families of Asian heritage.

On an early-morning walk with the kids, Franny saw a brown bunny zipping across the dirt campground road. She said, "Oh, that bunny must be adopted because it's brown." This wasn't exactly the message we had hoped she would take away from hanging out with other adoptive families. Still, it was undeniably astute and it blew us away coming from a seven-year-old. I worried that she was somehow getting the message that kids of colour were less wanted by their birth families. The truth is far more complex than could be explained to our children at that point.

Most of the families had adopted internationally, which is a very different route to creating a family from adopting through BC's foster-care system. Different because in my limited conversations with adoptive parents, it seems international adoption is the route to go if you want younger children and also children from a particular culture. A myth persists that international adopted kids are less likely to have medical conditions such as fetal alcohol spectrum disorder (FASD), though it seems, anecdotally, at least, that this is simply because there is less disclosure or less information available than in domestic adoptions. It appears there are higher instances of FASD from Russia and eastern European countries. There was a definite Christian flavour when talking to the families from the Okanagan, at least. Anecdotally, this seems to be true for domestic and international adoptive families. Many of the international adoption agencies were faith based. I remember attending an information session in Toronto about adopting from Guatemala using a Catholic agency; to our horror, we learned that there was a Catholic discount. If you could show you were Catholic, the Church would subsidize adoptions. Adoption seems to be a *good Christian* thing to do. I can only hope those families are adopting for the right reasons, because an adoptive child is wanted and not simply in service to their God. Who recruits? Not the gays.

At the adoptive families camping weekend, it also didn't help that our campsite was smack in the middle of the campground. We felt like we were in a fishbowl, while other veteran adoptive family campers staked their claim to quieter spots that they knew to be available on the perimeter. We put pressure on ourselves to overachieve as the only lesbian couple and, in fact, the only same-sex parents there. We participated in most activities, even leading some of them, and generally felt tired. I remember longingly listening to one of the dads, who slept in until late morning and seemed totally rested and relaxed on Saturday. We didn't fit in and we laboured over whether to leave early and got in a fight.

"Let's just go. I've had enough of this shit," Amy said.

"Let's stick it out. It's good for our kids," I answered.

"Our kids are fine, but they won't be if we are fighting."

"I'm embarrassed to leave. I mean, we are at an adoption camp and we can't fit in," I said.

"This is stupid. I need to get out of here and I don't care what they think," Amy said in a role reversal for us. No doubt everyone around heard us as our irritation, however much we lowered our voices, seeped through the tent-trailer mesh.

When it comes to adoption poster children, we too easily opt in to the trap that we are representing lesbians and gay men and we must excel. We must beat the heterosexuals at their own game. No pressure. I play the part. I am the '50s housewife with better food and no need for Valium. And a fulfilling job. And probably better sex because it is more reciprocal than I've been led to believe was the case for the average 1950s housewife. We are the gay couple in *American Beauty*—the only couple that is happy in that movie, tending to their garden, happily interacting with neighbours. In some ways, we are outdoing the traditional family. Some days I think it's a hell of a thing to aspire to, knowing what we know to be the downfalls of the nuclear family: overstressed parents, fewer numbers of caring adults, fewer opportunities to socialize with multi-generations and to integrate with all the kids in your neighbourhood.

No matter how much we fit in, we will never be the perfect family in many people's eyes, whether because we are a same-sex couple or because our brown kids are being raised by white parents. I'm not sure we want that but we are tired of it being thought of as some kind of disadvantage. Two parents loving their kids in a stable, loving home sounds idyllic to me. It scares the hell out of the homophobes. But I digress. There are far more accepting people than homophobes, especially in our corner of the world.

Recently, on Mother's Day, we were pleasantly surprised by good wishes not just from close friends, but from acquaintances too, a recognition that this is a special day around our house. And it was special, because our kids not only made us cards and breakfast in bed, scrambled eggs and tea and smoothies but also didn't whine when we asked them if we could go for a family hike. As we closed down Mother's Day 2019, we reflected that our first Mother's Day with the kids, when they were seventeen months old, was an exercise in endurance. We were up most of the night before with two feverish, puking toddlers. Still, we were grateful, even if it was through exhausted eyes on our couch.

Of all the labels we get assigned (e.g., transracial family with lesbian moms), most of all we are a family with young children. Tired in the way heterosexual couples are, juggling jobs, family life, house repairs, kids' soccer and music lessons, how to each fit in a workout and how to have some quality couple time, but nevertheless bemused with our children and the delightful and brilliant things they say.

Coming Out to Myself

I felt goosebumps and my stomach fluttered as I listened to Ms. Broadbear in our grade-ten health class at Napanee District Secondary School. "Homosexuals are people who are attracted to people of the same sex. Homosexuality is a lifestyle choice for a small percentage of humans. Homosexuals are often unhappy and society looks down on them." The gay gym teachers had to impart this lesson, without advocating for or outright condemning this "lifestyle." That homosexuality was taught at all was surprising, given its recent exclusion from the *DSM-III*, the third edition of the *Diagnostic and Statistical Manual of Mental Disorders*. It was no longer illegal either, though in no way was it presented as a viable, joyous option as, say, parenthood was. I ingested the air of shame. I got the message, that *those people* were freaks. This didn't stop me from having a flashback of watching Helen Reddy perform "I Am Woman" on a TV variety show when I was eight or so and feeling excited and attracted to her short sleek hair and spunky grin as she crooned about being invincible in her sultry, determined voice. Despite or perhaps because of the visceral memory of my first attraction, juxtaposed with the sting of the homosexuality lesson in health class, I was propelled to get a boyfriend and play sports fiercely. I buried this deep knowing in the pit of me because it simply couldn't be reconciled with my external reality.

The best thing that happened in high school is that we moved to Kingston. There I met people I still count as good friends, peers who were far more open minded and worldly, which turned out to be a precursor to coming out. I felt at home. My friends were ethnically diverse and listened to music beyond head-banging stuff that we used to get drunk to on the back roads of Napanee. This scene too often involved girls in the back of some souped-up Chevy, expected to lose their virginity. Once again I was saved by a move. Saved because I joined better sports teams and got into English writing courses with a caring and brilliant teacher, Mr. Kellway, who fostered my first attempts at poems. Angst-filled poems about thinly veiled sexuality. I broke up with my long-term boyfriend, a lovely guy, who still lived in Napanee.

When I was first starting to allow cracks of queer light to enter my consciousness, homosexuality hadn't long been off the books as a disease, and only a radical few had dared to think of it as an identity. It was especially hated by most of the mainstream, with lunchroom comments and op-ed musings such as "How dare they parade around? How dare they be proud?" This, with a backdrop of the Toronto bathhouse raids and the quiet murmur of gay bashings that went unreported to the untrustworthy police. I was desperate for a peer group that would be safe and help me find my way.

I was sowing the seeds of my eventual happiness in the sadness of what I thought were diminished possibilities. I never expected to marry legally; I never expected that we would even be able to express love in anything but a shrouded way. That we can declare our love and have the support of our friends and family is still something I don't take for granted.

I sought solace in music. I remember listening over and over to Bronski Beat's "Tell Me Why" and "Smalltown Boy," from the album *The Age of Consent*, before I was the age of consent. "The answers you seek will never be found at home." I remember my brother James blurting out one day, "Bronski Beat? They're all fags." I was mortified. I felt so ashamed yet also ablaze with a deep knowing as he brought this to my conscious awareness. From then on, I listened only on headphones or when my brother wasn't around.

My first choice for university was Waterloo, a hub of science and mathematics, though I would study kinesiology, which the math and engineering majors thought of as "bird courses." The school was young and ambitious and, at the time, had the best kinesiology program in the country. My senior biology teacher in high school encouraged me to consider this program, as did my senior health/physical education teacher. In the absence of much parental input, I took their advice. It was a huge bonus, too, that Waterloo was renowned for its co-op programs, which enabled students to more easily pay their way, with alternating academic and paid work terms. I also knew I wanted to go away to school, much to my parents' chagrin. Though I honed some drinking skills at uni, like most of my peers, I also changed the trajectory of my life. I was the first person in my extended family to get a degree and I never took for granted the opportunities it opened up for me.

✎

I first kissed a woman on my work term after my initial year of university, in the summer of 1986. It felt like seeing the world in colour for the first time. Unfortunately she was my boss and she was cheating on her partner so this just added an extra layer of shame to my virginal lesbian experience. There were more than a few times that I "worked extra hours" that summer. I would feel electric as I walked to meet her in various nooks in the sprawling former insane-asylum-cum-institution for developmentally delayed adults. Most frequently we met after hours in the "sheltered workshop," which was code for occupying unemployable adults with repetitive activities such as sanding blocks of wood until they were nothing but sawdust. As much as I knew it was wrong, I couldn't help myself each time, knowing that once I was in her arms, it felt utterly right.

I returned to Waterloo for second year and one of my best friends, Sheelah, and I promptly fell in love. It started as covert love often does, with a drunken kiss. It was the night of darkness and disguise, with me dressed as a wedge of cheddar cheese and her as a devil, head-to-toe red, with a pitchfork and all. After the costume party, we both leaned in and our lips met. Sparks flew. "This cardboard wedge of cheese makes it a little tough to be close," I said.

"It's okay. We'll figure it out," said Sheelah. Her devil costume somehow made it easier to kiss her, as if I could fool myself that I wasn't kissing a girl, as if it was her fault. She was a devil after all. We dismantled the cardboard cheese, wiped off her red makeup and made out the rest of the night in her room.

After Halloween, Sheelah and I spent an inordinate amount of time cocooning in her basement room, a whole new world of intimacy opening up to us, a world of tenderness and good sex and also of ideas. We felt a horrible sense of guilt when we ascended the basement stairs, often jolted into the world by the smell of boiling pasta, and re-emerged into the light of the kitchen in our shared house. It was painful to have falling in love commingled with such secrecy. We were forever on the lookout for opportunities to be alone, but always with an edge of fear and shame that our two other best friends, with whom we also lived, would find out.

I was astonished, then, a year later, to be entering the downtrodden Zehrs grocery store near the student ghetto as two women, one of whom I knew from class, were walking out. I heard one of them refer to the other one as "sweetie" and brush her hand as they gathered their groceries from the cart. I had never seen a public display or utterance of affection between women and it changed my world. It was the happiest grocery shop of my life, Kraft Dinner and canned tuna notwithstanding. I couldn't wait to tell my girlfriend that we weren't alone.

At that time, I never anticipated that coming out would be a lifelong process, like breathing. Instead I naively imagined it to be like birth. Dramatic, yes, but done once.

Even when we were out to our closest friends, we remained in the closet to everyone else. One night in third year, when Sheelah and I were living in different houses because of the complicated rental arrangements for co-op and non-co-op students, I ended up at her house. We snuck in late, after walking home from a party and stopping for a drunken snack, suicide wings, from the Huether Hotel. We slipped our spicy tongues into each other's mouths and then continued getting each other hot as our hands descended down our skin and into each other's pants. Our arousal quickly turned to pain. I'm sure her roommates awoke when we tried showering as a remedy (to no avail) but they were either too polite or drunk themselves to care. We were too ashamed to tell anyone or get help. We had to wait it out. I stayed over but we didn't get much sleep. I stung with shame in the morning as I finally came out of Sheelah's room into the kitchen, where her roommates were hanging out. I was desperate to make myself invisible and probably concocted some story about being too drunk to walk home from there, hence the sleepover. The suicide wings were nothing compared with the shame and secrecy splitting me in half. I slunk home.

> In her single bed, we touched,
> until the screech of saucy suicide—
> even sex's wetness could not repel
> Scotch Bonnet Pepper-laced touch.
> A visit to the hospital was out—
> mortification and fear ruled.
> We tried milk, heard it could dilute the oil.
> Time heals, so we waited it out,
> squinted into midday with bow-legged walks.
> I remember that pain, or was it the agony of the closet.
> Queers killing themselves rather than coming out.

BIRTH STORY

I attended a workshop about resilience in newborns shortly after we adopted the kids. It ended up just being a torment for parents whose children had less than a perfect start in life. Breastfeeding was assumed. Questions were asked about whether it was better to co-sleep, to have a water birth or a home birth. It felt so alienating to be in this room. Yet, despite so much transition and early trauma, our children were surviving and finding their way. It was difficult to reconcile the two realities.

A Pilates teacher of mine was about to give birth and was devastated to find out she had to have a C-section. "It's going to be okay," I told her. "Try and stay away from all those mothers going on about their perfect births. You are on a different path now."

"What do you mean?"

"That path of competitive glowing health, fretting over which organic product to feed their perfect babies, is oppressive." Perhaps it's my own response to my difficult start in life. I turned out okay despite nearly dying in childbirth, and my mother too. My mother was too sick to hold me for weeks. I was premature and not breastfed. I would have chosen to breastfeed if I could, absolutely, but I also think there is this weird competitiveness to all of the chatter. How can I make the perfect reproduction of myself? How can I give my babies every advantage so they can climb to the top of the child hill and win? Nobody would admit to this but it's what they are doing. It's why adoption is sometimes looked down on.

British Columbia's StrongStart program is designed to be a free, drop-in-style, positive early-learning experience for kids from birth to five years old. It was not meant to be competitive but sometimes you think it just might be. Success By 6, a government program aimed at positive early childhood development, gets amped up to success by six months. Perhaps we are not as far from our animal cousins as we think. Would we begrudge an armadillo for giving its offspring any competitive advantage? Perhaps it's all of us just trying to control what remains a very risky act for women—that of giving birth. It is often the most medically precarious moment women ever find themselves in.

I used to think the kids would learn about their birth mother and siblings in a single conversation and that would be that. I wasn't in denial enough to think it would be neat and tidy but I did think it would be over. Little did I know it is a work in progress—sort of like coming out, over and over again, throughout life, the same way we build a narrative of our lives, adding in context and experience. We've always been cautious about telling the twins certain facts about their history because some details about their birth family are hard and, once told, they can't be untold. Stories are fluid but sometimes they become roads we go down. The roads get paved and deeply grooved until we don't question the roads any longer at all and we find ourselves deep in despair. Yet we all have a deep need for story and we fill in whatever is left blank so we can understand and have some sort of release or closure. Stories serve our need at any given moment until external reality changes it.

One day, the kids said they wanted to play the "born game." I assumed my wife had played it with them when I was out. She assumed the same. Turns out they made it up themselves. The born game, as they called it when they were six or seven, was them playing out their story in a way that amazed us.

"I come out of Mom's tummy and Mama catches me." One at a time they lay between our legs as we took turns birthing and catching. They squealed with delight at this game. This went on for a while. Each of them mostly chose the mother they felt closest to, to be birthed by. When they emerged they let us hold them and look into their eyes with such love. It gutted me in the best way. It felt like a coronation of love. This was their new origin story.

This game they made up emerged after our family watched *E.T. the Extra-Terrestrial*, the movie where there is an alien from outer space and he wants to go home because he doesn't belong. Our son asked if his tummy-mummy lived in outer space. I was just glad he didn't think he was from outer space.

This is his story: that we birthed him. And his sister was so into it too, it was hard to know if they made it up together and sprang it on us or Franny just went along with Theo as if they had concocted it in both of their brains. Twin-genuity. I wrote about the born game in *Steeling Effects*.

Born Again

A family day together—
walk the dog, buy food and a leaf blower,
install storm windows,
play soccer on the sloping lawn,
eat pho in bowls and apples slathered in peanut butter,
cuddle in.
"Why does E.T. want to go home?"
> Theo once asked if his tummy-mummy lives in outer space.

"Why are the scientists doing all those tests on E.T.?"
> The twins were poked and prodded, observed, subject to
> developmental tests,

"Is E.T. dying because he needs love?"
> Post-placement, they stopped developing while they attached.
> Franny said adoption was like being kidnapped.

After the movie, Theo says, "Can we play the born game?"
The two moms get on the floor,
while the twins crawl out, pretending to be just born.
The moms take turns catching and birthing them,
the twins alternate who is born first.
The moms hold them and say,
you are loved;
we will care for you
and we are a forever family.
The seven-year-olds, all brown eyes and hope, gaze at their mothers,
newly born.

We weren't there at their birth, and perhaps story is all we ever have anyway. We weave facts into story. I love how Franny's origin story changes over time yet the thread of truth remains the same.

❧

On a sunny, unusually warm day in late March 1993, I parked my Ford Ranger truck and walked across our large snowy/muddy front yard outside of Picton, Ontario. I noticed the trickle of spring runoff from the farmer's fields that surrounded our corner lot. As I walked through the front door of this, the very first house I owned, a glimmer from the basement caught my eye.

I backed up and stepped down, squinting into the dark after the bright afternoon. The glimmer turned out to be from the silver gunwale of my canoe, which was floating around. I screamed and cried in our kitchen, reluctant to look again. I called my girlfriend, Sheelah, who was at work. "Our basement is totally flooded. Our canoe is floating around."

"Oh, Christ. Are you kidding?" she asked.

"No. There's like three feet of water down there. I can see gas on the surface of the water, probably from our lawn mower."

"Okay, I'll be there in an hour. Can you try and figure out where the water is coming from?" With her encouragement and reassurance that she was on her way, I got down to work. I walked down the wooden steps and reached for a paddle as it floated by, then I used the paddle to retrieve the empty canoe, floating eerily in the unfinished basement. I had to prevent the electric panel from being submerged. I overcame my fear of touching the panel while standing in a canoe, trying to reassure myself it would be safe but genuinely questioning what I knew of electricity. One wrong move and I would have been electrocuted. I turned off the main breaker and just for assurance all the breakers in the panel. I felt giddy with relief but my wet kinesiology notes floating by gave me a new challenge. The writing was now barely discernible; just three years out of school, I felt panic thinking I still needed those notes. I paddled around in the dark, wet basement, alone, overwhelmed by what to do about this huge issue, never having dealt with a flood or much of anything in my own home. Our foundation was likely ruined.

I called around for sandbags, realizing, with the help of a friend, that I needed to stop the flow of spring runoff. I finally found a gravel place that picked up. "Hello. Yes, I need sandbags," I said.

"What for?" asked the dude.

"A whole farmer's field of spring runoff is flooding my basement through a basement garage."

The guy said, "Ha. You don't need sand; you need a dyke."

I started laughing and couldn't stop. *We've got two of us here and it isn't helping.* I didn't say that out loud. Sheelah wondered what the heck was so funny. The tears rolled down my face as I mustered a response. "Yeah, you are probably right. I need a dyke," I answered.

Sheelah and I spent until about midnight digging a diversion ditch, slowly redirecting the flow. We had to break through ice underneath the superficial runoff that was still flowing, and it was a work against time before it refroze as the temperature plummeted without the spring sun. In what seemed a miracle at the time, the basement water was mostly gone by the next day.

Once we stopped the flow, it drained quickly through the sandy floor of our unfinished basement. This would end up being an apt metaphor for my own emotional healing, at the time, shoring up my foundation though I felt out of my depth—diverting the flow and creating new pathways.

It's been decades since this happened, though I've told the story to my kids. Still, I worry that they see only this confident, capable person whom they can't live up to. They not only didn't see my fight but have no idea there was a struggle. Maybe this is a downside of having kids later—I've worked out the core of my emotional baggage and they think I've got it together. My kids have so many more resources, in part because I am more resourced to parent them, because I worked hard at healing.

The Courage to Heal was my bible when I was healing from sexual abuse. It gave me a road map of how to name shame and work with it rather than holding it like a hot potato or walking miles not to feel it. It was dark and I was lost at first, then I started to feel my own heartbeat, then I caught a glimpse of light here and there and found my way.

I will be hopefully handing my children flashlights for their dark moments. I think they have to find their own but this answer sits uneasily. It does take courage to heal. May they have strength and insight. I had a deep inner voice when I was in my twenties. I imagine it came from my grandmother, who loved me unconditionally. I have a hunch that my children will internalize some healthy voices. I'm not sure. Who the hell is sure? I couldn't have known from my life in my twenties that I would have turned out to have such a good life. I take solace in reading my train-wreck journals from my twenties. I had boundary issues with friends and lovers; I didn't know how to be alone. I pulled myself up with the help of many and I really started to believe that I was worthy. I started to believe that I deserved good things and I didn't sabotage my life so much. It is reassuring to see this arc. I somehow want my kids to see that I wasn't always this way. I had lots of doubt and troubles.

I have some hope that their brains will rewire themselves through adolescence, that all the prefrontal cortex development will be a welcome respite from the amygdala's reign. Hopefully, having ten good years of stability and love within their family will impact the rewiring. It's the story I'm telling myself at the moment. I wonder if one can accompany anyone else on his or her journey? If so, a case can be made for our twins accompanying each other.

We were recently talking to Franny about her birth mom because it was that time of year to write her a letter. She was talking about not having her birth mom around, not being able to meet her, and we asked how that felt. Franny said, "That's okay. I have both of you and most of the time you are fun."

I love that kid and she's going to break our hearts when she journeys out alone.

COMING OUT TO MY PARENTS

I'd come out to eight friends in a row in my third year at university. Eight friends had, in turn, come out to me. I felt I needed to come out to my parents because my girlfriend, Sheelah, was moving in with me for a four-month work term in Ottawa and it felt too duplicitous not to. I was being ripped in half. I later told one of my friends that I didn't want to tell my parents out of fear they would also come out to me, but that joke protected me from the fear that I would be shunned.

The first lesbian-content book I could get my hands on, *Lesbian Nuns: Breaking Silence*, fuelled my curiosity about queer life and its seeming confinement to the closet. Buoyed by the anonymity of being far from home and university, I went to Coles in Sault Ste. Marie in search of any lesbian content I could find. The stories in *Lesbian Nuns* were riveting for a third-year student on a co-op work term in highly visible positions as both a residence don and an athletic co-ordinator at Sault College. I gobbled up every word of the book again and again with my door locked and curtains drawn. *Lesbian Nuns* lived under my mattress the rest of the time and once or twice had to be quickly put away when a student knocked on my door looking for advice or simply homesick and needing company. Though I had no intention of taking a vow of chastity, there were validating tales in the book. There seemed to be few choices for a nun: split yourself in two and lead a very closeted life in the convent, or leave your vocation and community.

I came out to my family over Christmas holidays in third year, because all the coming-out books I could get my hands on suggested you do it when you can hang around together, so they can see you as a person. I was sitting on the stairs that ascended from the cathedral-ceilinged living room to the bedrooms in our suburban Kingston backsplit. The Christmas tree was adorned with coloured lights and tinsel just in my peripheral vision, my mother across the room in their swankiest chair, reupholstered in a butterscotch ripple pattern after the black leather ripped. My father was standing up at the bottom of the stairs and my brothers were not around, which is why I chose that moment to unburden myself. "I'm gay." (I couldn't utter the word *lesbian* to my parents.) "Sheelah is not just my friend; she's my girlfriend."

My mother said, "No, not Sheelah. She got our dog drunk." It was true, she did, at my surprise twenty-first birthday party that my parents had organized with all my friends. I too was pissed off at this out-of-character-act by my secret girlfriend.

"Yeah, that was unfortunate. But, you know, she is awesome in other ways." If my girlfriend was someone who didn't get the dog drunk, would it have been easier? I was kind of relieved and dismayed by the distraction, *I'm gay* still reverberating through me.

My mother choked out "We love you." We hugged and my mother and I cried. My father bit his lip and said nothing. Christmas was subdued as they went through the motions, their heartbreak just barely below the surface. They seemed in shock and took no obvious joy in any of the usual Christmas activities. I felt relieved at no longer holding this secret that had ripped me apart to hold. I felt intense relief that they were able to reassure me of their love in that moment and that my biggest fear did not come true. I also slunk around the house that Christmas break, feeling guilty and responsible for their obvious heartbreak. It was very difficult to hold the range of emotion and I felt relief leaving for Ottawa after the break.

Our weekly phone calls through the winter steered well clear of the topic. At most, they would ask what Sheelah was up to and I would regale them with funny stories about her tribulations as a new graduate with a general science degree. She got a job selling dictionaries door to door. My parents still have the oversized dictionary: a fat, fake, gilded dinosaur. We talked about sports a lot. I probably emphasized my important job working for Health Canada.

Later my mother said, "It was our issue to get over, not yours." They talked to their friends. Their friends were left-leaning liberals. I don't think any of them would have wanted a gay kid themselves but they sure showed up for my parents and indirectly for me. I felt very fortunate, knowing some of my friends weren't so lucky.

Sheelah and I went out with my classmates frequently, for many of us wound up in Ottawa for our four-month work terms that winter. After a drunken night, which probably ended at the Lafayette House, the hole in the wall in the ByWard Market that served quarts of Molson Canadian or Labatt 50, one of our friends, Monica, staggered home with us on frozen but well-plowed sidewalks. The sidewalks were always well plowed in the nation's capital, it seemed, despite it being the coldest and snowiest winter I can recall. So closeted was I that Monica slept with me in the double bed and Sheelah slept on the pullout couch in the living room. It was perverse. Even drunk, I felt sick about it and barely slept. I wonder, now that my sexual orientation is no secret, if Monica ever looks back at that and wonders, *What the hell?* I had so much shame, it's hard to feel now, though sometimes I still feel this inheritance in my chest: *If I don't take up too much space, perhaps I can survive.*

Coming out to my parents slowly freed me to be myself. They gradually grew to understand I was the same person I'd always been. That we can declare our love and have the support of our friends and family is still something I don't take for granted. When I was coming out, my story of myself (straight) was at odds with the self I was unveiling (lesbian). Becoming me was a process of accepting myself gradually. Revisions take time. Any writer will tell you that revision is a dangerous process, where, in the fog of our own lives, we may mistakenly cut really important passages or leave out essential details.

Identifying as a lesbian, a horizontal identity, in that it is not shared with your family of origin necessarily, is so different from those vertical identities that are handed down and within which you can feel a sense of belonging, e.g., Indigenous or Latino. My parents had to grieve the loss in their story—they thought it would mean no grandkids from me, and my mother grieved that.

Flip ahead thirty years and I have had a couple of poems on BC Transit; a captive audience of bus commuters in Vancouver get to read about me coming out. This is better than I ever imagined in my twenties and only slightly vulnerable. It is heartwarming for me to hear from people whose lives are opened up by reading poems about coming out. Amy and I talk to our kids about being lesbians. We talk about not having equal rights when we were coming out. They think it's silly and inconceivable we weren't treated fairly. They just don't understand what the deal is. Coming out is a lifelong process, not a one-off. Breathing, not birth. When we originally came out we were under the mistaken impression it would be finished with after that one difficult conversation.

An excerpt from my poem "Come Out," in *Acquired Community*:

I was righteous, thought I had come out.
I'd told my high school friends, my parents, my aunt by then.
I celebrated in the streets with my friends,
eight of us in solid-coloured shirts,
walked in rainbow formation,
Made the cover of *Xtra*.
In my naiveté, I thought I was done.

Twenty years later, I'm still doing it,
the only thing I want to have come out of is my mother's womb.
Not to the kindergarten teacher, the triage nurse,
the dentist, the law clerk, the adoption worker,
or the posh woman in the condo elevator
who asks, *Which one of you is the mom?*
then turns to press any button she can
when I say, *We both are.*

It's like breathing, not birth.

Amplified Parenting

In grade five our twins had assignments on simple machines. Simple machines are screws, inclined planes, wedges, wheels and axles, and pulleys. They had to integrate three simple machines in solving a problem of their own creation. My son is very mechanically minded but he has little confidence in his ability to come up with a solution to a problem. He didn't really understand the assignment. He quickly grew frustrated, throwing up his arms and almost flinging an iPad across the dining room table, and said, "I'm stupid."

"You are so not stupid. You teach us how to fix things around here. Let's look at some examples of simple machines online."

"I don't care. I am no good." I know it took years to turn down the volume of my own self-critical voice, to replace it with something better. It still fools me sometimes. Denying it was not how I overcame it. Telling it I understand and "Thank you for protecting me" is far more useful. It reminds me of an Audre Lorde poem, "Coping," that has stuck with me over the years because I used it to encourage my dispirited self as I healed:

Young seeds that have not seen the sun
Forget
and drown easily.

"You have a bully inside of you. I will not let your inner bully beat you up with that voice." He looked at me, half understanding and cynical.

"I hate myself." In what seemed like hours later, we got past his destructive voice to the assignment. He used a large log, an incline plane, a wheelbarrow and an axe to solve the issue of heating a home with logs in the cold Canadian winter when the logs are too heavy to lift and too large to put in a wood stove. We videotaped it and he explained it with command in his voice. He had to get out of his own way to do this. While it felt like a victory in our household, this project also left Amy and me sad and exhausted.

I understand where this voice originates. It is a coping mechanism for powerlessness. *I'm no good* is a handy alternate explanation for adoption-related abandonment. I have a hunch that this is deep-seated self-loathing because he was taken from his biological mom at birth. Who could come to terms with that level of rejection? *Was it something I did?* is still easier to accept than total powerlessness. One way his story can be understood is abandonment by his birth mom and then by foster parents when he was fourteen months old. Another way it can be understood, and this is my hope for him: everyone has loved him along the way and it took him longer than usual to find his way to his forever family, but he did nothing wrong.

In her CBC piece on amplified parenting, "Adoption Is Not Like It Is in the Movies," Paula Schuck writes that parenting adopted kids is "bigger, harder, brighter, louder, more heartbreaking and sometimes more rewarding than raising a child you gave birth to." She couldn't have more accurately described our family. I had an aha moment. Our family started with a loss. We collectively hold the twins' grief and trauma of losing their birth mother and then their foster parents when adopted by us. We will be a container for their early trauma until they are able to hold it themselves as adults. We have told them pieces of their story that we feel they can manage in ways they have the resilience to hear. This is an art form and one we labour over. My story, for a long time, was that my children had the best possible start given that they were with one foster family who took care of their every need and loved them. Perhaps my version of the story is as true as the traumatic story of the twins losing both their birth mother and their foster parents within the first fourteen months of their lives, but I am only just learning to hold that much divergent truth at once. It is little wonder that the Ministry of Children and Family Development considers every adopted child to be "special needs." Adoption loss is subtle. It is not like some confirmed diagnosis. This fact has come home to roost. It is an uneasy habitation.

We've also learned that our children's neurological pathways are more worn as a result of trauma. What for you or me may be a slight stressor sends them into fight or flight more quickly. We were tasked with being their scaffolding, meaning safely supporting our kids while they grow into and beyond their losses. When asked if we could take these children, we said yes. We didn't know what we were getting into, just like the rest of humanity when they say yes to parenthood. I do think our kids need more scaffolding than kids without "trauma pathways." I have been a parent for ten years as I write this. My arms are more conditioned to hold them up now but sometimes they are also more tired.

Parenting kids with early trauma can be heartbreaking. Preverbal trauma equates with diffuse sabotage. It looks like unexplained rage, like throwing an ottoman across a room because you can't find your belt. It looks like a scorched-earth policy if you feel betrayed, screaming the most hurtful things you can at the ones who love you. If we go a day without a trauma outburst, we are relieved and grateful. I think it comes back to loss, to early loss, that could be construed as rejection. When they are in terror there is no reassuring my children. It is shocking and heartbreaking for us to be able to do little about it, other than ensure they don't hurt themselves and hope it will dissipate in the long run, that they will learn to trust us and that they will come out the other end. Resilience-building in action is very difficult to witness. Necessarily there is suffering. That is why so many people don't adopt. My kids have learned more than I wish anyone to ever know of resilience. They know it in their bones, or wherever body memories are held within us. It is very hard to sit with for longer than a minute or two, despite my own deep reflections on trauma from childhood sexual abuse and healing from shame. This is the kind of contemplation that shallows my breath and makes me need to move suddenly to shake the amount of suffering and deep-seated pain that they have felt acutely and will navigate throughout their lives as a result of loss upon loss from their adoption experiences.

According to *The Primal Wound: Understanding the Adopted Child*, by Nancy Newton Verrier, when separation from the birth mother occurs, adopted children have lower body temperatures, more cortisol, fewer endorphin receptors and less sensitivity to endorphins. Cue the endorphin-laden activities. For us this included the primacy of parent-child bonding time with one of us as a full-time parent for the first three years after we brought them home. It continues to include lots of family activities: swimming, walks and beach time.

We've both done a bucketload of counselling too, dragging our weary bodies in to a kind, empathic therapist, crying in front of healers who kindly say in various ways that "there is no magic pill" when we talk about how the kids so easily go fight, fright or flight. Their remedies are self-care, love and connection with our children. Our tears were perhaps all just letting go of the hope of a quick fix to their deep trauma. We must not be doing things right because they are in pain, we thought.

The biggest relief I got from counselling was that it was a container for our own grief as parents. A place we could go to share our doubts and our challenges with holding it all. Oh, sure, prescribed games such as chess that work on impulse control and building dwellings together with Popsicle sticks were helpful. We followed through with a suggestion to put tons of photos of all our children's important people on our walls so they could be reminded of all the people who love them. Our family portraits fill the stairway up to our bedrooms. Photos of their siblings and birth mother greet them when they walk in their rooms. A punching bag was up for a while but they never used it, preferring to use us instead when deeply triggered.

The first trip to our family doctor in Nelson ended in tears. The kids, who were just sixteen months old or so, were obviously afraid of newness and did not want to be held by anyone but us. They freaked out when the doctor gently examined them. He cut the exam short in favour of the long game of developing a relationship with them and didn't want to add to their obvious distress. He counselled us that their mild developmental delay might be temporary but it might be permanent too. The family doctor referred us to the pediatrician for a consultation as Theo had a hernia above his belly button, a toonie-sized molehill bubbling beneath his skin. He warned us that it would likely need to be operated on at BC Children's Hospital in Vancouver, an eight-hour journey each way for us.

Our visit with the pediatrician yielded a reassurance that the hernia would diminish over years and naturally disappear. No intervention was necessary, nor was he at any risk of a rupture. She said his abdominal wall would strengthen over time and she had no concerns. The specialist also informed us that he did not have fetal alcohol spectrum disorder, given his ability to connect and focus. While this was not foremost on our minds, it was a niggle in the back of our brains, despite reassurances from the neonatal health-care team. I came away from that consultation with the pediatrician with tears of relief rolling down my cheeks.

I like to think that Theo's trauma is like his hernia, that it will diminish over time as he strengthens and gets more flexible. That as much as we would like to surgically remove trauma, it is not to be fixed in this dramatic way. Our hope is that he will grow strong and the trauma will be in the rear-view mirror and nothing will get ruptured in the interim. Then there are those moments when he is in terror or he is saying "I hate myself" and we *do* yearn for a knife to cut out the rancour instead of waiting for the healing of his ruptured attachment.

SPORTY GIRLS
AND SEEDY BARS

Being a fierce competitor in sports was a beautiful respite from not feeling good enough or feminine enough in the rest of my life. I was shocked that I made the varsity badminton team at the University of Waterloo. I had very little sense of my own skill, a situation that I attribute to shame but also to a generational phenomenon that many working-class people share, including my parents: *Who do you think you are? Don't stand out.* I left Waterloo as an outstanding graduating athlete.

I bunked with my teammate Anne on overnight road trips to badminton tournaments; funds were tight for such a low-profile varsity sport and everyone shared double beds in mediocre motels. We slept a few inches apart. I could hear her breathing slow as she drifted off to sleep. I was certain she was more at peace with herself than I was. By bedtime we'd both showered after our respective days of competition. She always smelled clean, fresh but not perfumy. I often went to sleep worrying about coming out or silently crying about a fight I'd had with my girlfriend. The necessary compartmentalizing of our lives meant we occupied solitary worlds. It was only after graduation that Anne and I ran into each other, to our astonishment, at the Rose, a lesbian bar in Toronto. We could have supported each other through those years of gruelling daily practices, of quiet road trips staring out the window, both fretting over coming out. All the times I was forlorn because of the split between falling deeply in love for the first time, with Sheelah, and pretending to be just friends. Instead we lay beside each other in parallel loneliness. My first concern when I noticed Anne at the Rose was that she was going to out me, until I realized that she was in a dyke bar too. We had a bittersweet embrace on the dance floor.

Going to straight bars in the 1980s always involved a deep edge of fear about two legitimate possibilities: (1) getting beaten up for slipping in a tipsy kiss with a lover in a moment of indiscretion, and (2) being sexually assaulted by drunken men wanting to *teach us a lesson*. Entering and exiting women's bars in the 1980s also had an edge of danger, one we were willing to withstand. Most of the bars were entered through a maze or an unmarked metal door in an alley or, in the case of the Coral Reef in Ottawa, a parking garage, where men in cars might first harass us before we found the elusive door. The entrance through the Plaza Hotel in Kingston, the penitentiary capital of Canada, was even worse. You had to walk through the recently released prisoner / biker / strip bar on the main level and go up a set of back stairs. Not one bit of it felt safe and I'm sure we stayed longer because we couldn't face the catcalls from the ex-cons when leaving the bar, which got worse as the night wore on. Even if the entrances were not disguised, as at the Rose on Parliament Street, we'd all scan for drunken straight men hanging around the entrance or just a little down the block, out of reach of the butchy bouncers.

Fortunately I was not part of the frequent homophobic incidents around the bar. My girlfriend and I did get "fucking dykes" yelled at us by some guys passing by in a car as we walked across the Bloor viaduct on the way home from an evening out. Though nothing came of it, we were rattled for the remainder of our long walk home, and we were conscious not to make any body contact, wondering if the car full of men would return and make our lives hell. The slur echoed in my mind for many weeks and built on my brother James's similar yelled sentiment to me a few years prior. "Fucking dyke," he yelled at me at the front door of my parents' house.

"Yeah, I am. So what?" I stood my ground as he went outside. This and all the other insults together formed the homophobic chorus that was the backdrop of my life in the 1980s and '90s.

Going through the front door of a club was both liberating and vulnerable. No wonder some women drank so much. It was a thrill, once inside, to see yourself in others, to see women dancing together, whether it was two butchy women holding another in close to Melissa Etheridge's "You Can Sleep While I Drive," or women dancing in groups to "Gonna Make You Sweat" by C+C Music Factory. In the bars, I associated the smell of women's sweat, without the linger of men's aftershave, as safe. I felt free, without the worry of being hit on, let alone assaulted, by any men. Still, many of us felt vulnerable if we were not *out* in the rest of our lives and we encountered women who were. It was the old downtowner versus uptowner issue. Downtowners were women who couldn't pass in the world and by default were *out*. Many had marginalized jobs and lives. Uptowners, often professionals, came downtown on weekends and the rest of the week were closeted and relatively privileged. People who were more *out* were dangerous because they had nothing to lose.

Besides the bar, my respite in the early '90s was gay sports leagues. On Saturday mornings, I played Pink Turf soccer in Withrow Park. The park was lined by three-storey brick homes, gentrified or in the process of gentrification at the time. The homes, and the lives of the yuppies that inhabited them, strolling with their lattes and Chariot strollers, seemed so far out of reach, all we could do was deride them. We told ourselves we never wanted to be married with children. *Have fun, suckers* was our sentiment toward the women and we even voiced it aloud from the safety of the soccer pitch. Meanwhile, we enjoyed easy conversations with each other without the daily vigilance of changing the pronoun of our girlfriends, or saying Allen instead of Ellen, as was the case when talking with colleagues or straight acquaintances.

We also worked out unresolved issues with our exes on the field or defended against women who had rejected us from the bar. I once played against an ex as her girlfriend watched from the sidelines. In a weird twist, her girlfriend was also my ex and the only person to break my heart, up to that point at least.

"Rosie, pass me the ball."

"What are you doing all the way back here?"

"C'mon. Just give it to me."

"Okay, okay."

I dribbled the ball past their forwards, then around their midfielders, picking up speed as my teammates called for the ball and then sort of slowed down and watched me. With a glance toward my ex-girlfriend on the sidelines, I deked around one more fullback and hauled off with the strength of all my determined fury. I propelled the ball, piercing the air between the goalkeeper's outstretched arms, into the top of the net. My stunned teammates flocked toward me as we did our victory march back to centre field for another kickoff.

"Holy shit. What got into you?"

"A little fuck you to a couple of my exes that are here."

"Maybe we can invite your exes to all of our games."

After soccer, our team would usually go out for brunch on the nearby Danforth. The Danforth neighbourhood was a funny mix of yuppies and old

Greeks, the early immigrants to the area. We would take over a large table in a restaurant and be *out* and brash for a while in a neighbourhood in which we felt relatively anonymous. Eventually we all went home, showered and readied ourselves to go to the bar. It seemed especially cruel that some of my friends had to so quickly step back into the closet in between soccer and dancing if they lived with their families of origin, but it was a vast improvement to having no bars to go to, no sports leagues to play openly in, as had been the case a handful of years earlier.

The Rose had a patio, albeit with a very high fence. Still, it felt like a revelation to be out in the open air at a dyke bar, dancing to our anthems: "I Will Survive," "Rise Up" and "High School Confidential." We channelled all the lesbians who historically never had this privilege and in that way dancing was a political as well as a personal act.

I met my wife playing in the Rainbow Hoops basketball league in 2003. Each game was infused with the competitive spirit and camaraderie of women who had so often been shunned in other arenas.

My posse of dear friends insisted on brunch so they could interview her, all six of them. "Will your friends be nice to me?" she asked. I laughed.

We went to Edward Levesque's in Leslieville. After playing twenty questions in the long lineup, we sat at the back in the mezzanine overlooking the open kitchen. My friend Sharon, an archivist, handed Amy an application form to fill out. "We know everything there is to know about all of us. This is all about you," she said.

"Okay then. What do I need to say to make my case? I think Jane is awesome. I have only good intentions. I moved here from Boston but I'm from St. Louis."

"Are you using Jane to get citizenship?"

"No. I'm a landed immigrant. I've already applied for citizenship."

"So you plan on sticking around? You aren't taking Jane to live in Boston, are you?"

"I'm not planning on moving back to be closer to George W., if that's what you are asking."

"And I hear you did your master's at Harvard?" asked Cathy, while the rest of the committee were suitably impressed.

"Who is a better basketball player, you or Jane?" asked another of my friends.

"Jane got traded to our team to help us out because we were losing every game."

I piped up, "It's about the chemistry. We pass really well together."

"Amy, did you play a varsity sport?"

"I played field hockey at Colgate."

"Are you out to your family? If so, how are they about everything?"

"I'm out. My family are Midwest Republicans. They aren't marching in Pride parades but they deal with it. They've come a long way."

"Eggs or pancakes?"

"You'll soon find out," said Amy.

I loved hearing her husky Melissa Etheridge voice and easy laugh as she navigated the grill session. I enjoyed guessing correctly that she'd go for eggs rather than something sweet. A decade later than Pink Turf soccer, and where we ate brunch was a matter of choice, knowing that wherever we landed in downtown Toronto would be safe and we'd be beyond reproach. In ten years we'd come a long way, baby.

For our tenth wedding anniversary, Amy and I visited New York City in 2016. A pilgrimage to the Stonewall Inn felt like stepping back in time, the original draft beer still soaked in the ratty rug. The archival photos lining the tobacco-stained walls told a story of gay pioneers who were willing to die to get respect. I honoured the history and gave gratitude to our predecessors who put up with police raids in a bar run by the mob in order to socialize and to find love. Then we sat on a patio of our choice and raised a glass without regard for the sexual orientation of our neighbours packed onto the Lower Manhattan patio. We regarded the gay pioneers, gave thanks and made plans.

SPECIAL

I've spent most of my career helping people with disabilities and injuries to overcome barriers to employment. One of the things I've gleaned from this is that people who have no choice embrace their disabilities and assistive technologies more readily than people who can sometimes get by using regular tools. A quadriplegic, for example, will usually be more successful at embracing and using voice-input technology than someone with sore wrists. If they want to compose on a computer, they must use their voice, not their hands, so they get proficient at it. Someone with mild carpal tunnel syndrome may try voice input but get frustrated by the learning curve or initial accuracy rate and revert to their traditional keyboard, putting up with discomfort and other symptoms in order to get their work done efficiently.

My kids pass as kids without special needs. They rarely act out in public, so health-care providers, counsellors, teachers and even friends are surprised when we bring up trauma and in particular the designation "special needs." It was not something we were willing to say out loud early on, despite the Ministry of Children and Family Development's designation. Part of the issue may originate from the term itself. We live in an era in which everyone seems to want their kids to be special. It's why, in our town, we have parents flocking toward, and hence waiting lists for, any program that is labelled "alternative." Many people moved here as an alternative to the draft, the rat race or conformity, to access alternative medicine or to live communally. It is a fine line between recognizing that each child is different and responds to different parenting strategies, perhaps, and feeding each kid a steady diet of "You are exceptional."

Our children have trauma. We thought love was enough. Love gets you a long way; however, it doesn't get you certification in rerouting a brain with a superhighway to the amygdala and its associated freaking out, extreme tantrums and unexplained rage. I've often characterized our parenting journey as a huge rewiring project, and we didn't start out as electricians.

A couple of years ago, the kids both exploded in rage. I don't even recall why but one set the other off. We would normally get a handle on it by separating and calming them but they were beyond that. Both of us were yelling. "Stop breaking things. Settle down. Stop freaking out. Stop yelling!" I heard each of us say, "I can't do this."

Our neighbour came over after seeing me crying out on our deck. She hugged me and said, "I'll talk to the kids. You guys should take a break." We were both so wrecked after this double-trauma whammy. As is too often the case in such extremely stressful times, Amy and I get in fights, screaming out our own stress at each other.

I am disappointed by the number of people who refuse the notion of adoption as a special need or those who like to pretend that a few years of good parenting obviates early-life trauma. I try to understand what compels someone who has not been through adoption to state that any kid can have tantrums or rage, and challenge how we know it's related to adoption? It is to dismiss their loss as trivial. In my generous moments, I think it is people seeking to reassure us that the kids are all right or are going to be all right. They want to believe that love is enough, akin to being colour blind when it comes to race. I wanted to believe that love is enough too. I still believe that love goes a very long way, that it is essential, but I don't think it is everything. Perhaps it's a tendency for some adoption advocates who are working hard to shed stigma around mental health and adoption correlations—an attempt to normalize the impact adoption may have.

I am equally forlorn over those who say "Children are resilient" when talking about early-life trauma. What goes unsaid is the expectation that they will get over it. I feel infuriated by this dismissal. It sounds like an excuse that would come out of Conservative politicians to defend unconscionable cuts to education or meal programs for children and separating undocumented children from their parents. If you think that children are unaffected by sep-aration from their mother, then perhaps when your next child is born, try leaving them at the hospital for two weeks, and try not holding them when you get home. I count among my closest friends those who are able to listen and acknowledge our reality without minimizing or catastrophizing it.

There are those who reveal their biases about adopted kids, assuming they have or will have mental health issues. The stigma of adoption is real but subtle. It's rather like homophobia these days, at least in Canada. Not many people are burning rainbow flags and taking baseball bats to queers but all kinds of assumptions are made about us based on our membership in a group: lesbian and gay relationships don't last, lesbians hate men, two men can't raise children. The list of myths for special-needs adoptions is there, though often unspoken, or couched in concern on behalf of the speaker to the adoptive parents: adopted kids are extra trouble, they will end up in jail, they will use drugs, they will break your hearts, your partnership won't last. All I can say is that in our family we do a lot to foster emotional and mental well-being. We are careful with whom we talk about our "scaffold" issues, the need to provide extra support for our kids because of underlying trauma. We feel some obligation to be a poster family for adoption and lesbian and gay parenting. No pressure!

Amy and I take respite, yes, from the usual hectic pace, the sibling fights, the need to care for others. We also take respite from those deep-rage episodes that leave us raw and shaken. And perhaps respite from feeling like we hold ourselves to some higher standard because we are being watched. This usually looks like having the kids looked after by someone they know well and us going away for a couple of nights. I guess we would drop them off at their grandparents' if their grandparents lived close. The kids look forward to this break, especially when it is with beloved friends. The last respite weekend we had, the kids got their own fancy rooms at a friend's house. They got to pick their favourite foods, went to the hot springs and got way more screen time than we would give them. It was no doubt a respite for our children from us as well. And we modelled for them what it means to take care of a relationship. Meanwhile Amy and I finished conversations, lay on the couch and watched a movie in the middle of the afternoon, had romantic dinners and generally remembered how much we enjoy each other's uninterrupted company.

We pass as a highly functional family. We are, in many respects, and we are well resourced. It is surprising to some of our friends, then, when we take respite time. I was horrified recently to hear a teacher complaining that he worked with kids who were so difficult that the parents got respite time and money from the government.

Yes, that is us. We get post-adoptive assistance money that pays for therapy and respite care. Our respite time is time to regroup without redirecting behaviour, without being vigilant and managing a triggered kid. It is an opportunity to fill our own buckets back up so we can enter the land of helping our kids to manage their amplified feelings every day.

Pride... in the Name of Love

The prelude to my first-ever Pride Day was a heated argument with my girlfriend, Sheelah. She laughed when she heard the parade route, guffawed that the gays would be taking over downtown Toronto and dismissed it as a bad idea, a good way to make a spectacle. Underneath all of this was fear that her mother, who had recently left the United Church when they decided to ordain homosexual ministers, would see her.

I marched. Sheelah stood anonymously in a crowd on a sidewalk at Yonge and Bloor. That she waved at me was a big step. I was simply floored that I was with a hundred thousand others, celebrating and showing our faces. I never dreamed there were so many others and that collectively we could stand up. It was 1992 and Pride Day was the biggest antidote to my own shame. I was so focused on not standing out with my colleagues and with my family that I couldn't quite get my head around the drag queens on floats or the boy toys in tighty-whiteys dancing behind trucks sponsored by gay bars. I was not quite ready to embrace the movement, so up my own ass was I. I thought the frivolity of gay men's appearances was over the top and embarrassing. I have since realized how much courage it must have taken to be so out when their friends were dropping dead around them, with no cure in sight and little political will to stop the AIDS epidemic, despite hundreds of thousands of deaths at that point already in North America alone. I respect living large, especially now that I understand that shame will never be an effective strategy for acceptance, nor will acquiescence.

The next year, a gang of us rented a twelve-person van and drove to a KOA campground in the suburbs of Washington, DC. We took the Metro downtown and marched on Washington for lesbian and gay rights with a million others. Martina Navratilova blew me away talking so openly about discrimination. She stood up and lost hundreds of thousands of dollars in endorsements as a result. The Indigo Girls identified publicly as "allies" but at least they performed at the concert after the march. Cybill Shepherd spoke publicly—apparently they'd asked dozens of celebrities before she said yes. It didn't matter that her speech was pithy. ACT UP had vigils and surrounded the White House because of Bill Clinton's inaction and backtracking on equal rights. It was my first time seeing the AIDS quilt. Its breadth and heart left me speechless and sobbing. Each square of the quilt made by lovers or sometimes family was such an intimate outpouring of love and grief, and panels sewn together seemed to amplify the grief to a level that seemed apt for the scale of loss, at a time when words could not do justice to the magnitude of loss and wilful neglect. No political speech, however powerful, could ever touch the quilt in poignancy. And it was a quilt, a homemade object meant to protect, to nurture family members through frigid nights.

The most vulnerable Pride parade I went to was in my hometown of Kingston, Ontario. One couldn't mingle in with millions of others. At most there were a hundred marchers and I was bound to be seen by people I knew from high school who would have no allegiance to talking about me respectfully. The Pride parade was followed by a Shriners parade. Hence there was a large but very confused crowd lining Princess Street as hardbodies and drag queens donning Carmen Miranda hats were replaced by men with large girths wearing fezzes and riding mini-motorbikes.

I cried every year as I watched the Pride flag being hoisted onto the side of the 519 Community Centre on Church Street in Toronto from my thirtieth-floor office at Yonge and Bloor. Pride parades ballooned from one hundred thousand to one million people in the '90s and from a weekend to a week of celebrations. One year, my friends and I each marched in a T-shirt of a different solid colour from the rainbow spectrum. Collectively we made a rainbow and we made the cover of *Xtra*. It felt validating, for most of the images that made the paper were dramatic: the drag queens, the bears, dykes on bikes. Attracting attention and being on the cover of a newspaper felt vulnerable but I felt so free, so delighted to be present and marching with friends. I felt like I belonged. I cried at the promise that we could be equal, for it was still a distant promise.

Then there was the Dyke March, from which I also drew strength. It was like coming home, to be among thousands of dykes whose causes I felt most aligned to and in whom I saw myself when I looked at all the short-haired, tough and tender marchers. I don't often miss Toronto these days, living in the middle of the mountains, but I do miss Pride Week. I miss mingling with hot bodies on Church Street, seeing LGBT performers on stage and the dyke dance.

Despite the brash parades once a year, in the early '90s I also found myself nervously walking down the long corridor to human resources at my first full-time job as a graduate, working for the provincial government. It was summer and the breeze coming through the open windows at the sprawling institution on the old grounds of a World War II army base in Picton, Ontario, provided intermittent relief from the heat. I had a mission: getting my uninsured partner extended health benefits before she had to get dental work. I took a deep breath as I turned into the HR office. "Hi, Ina. I want to change my benefits. Is Sandra in?"

"Sure. I'll see if she's free." Ina ushered me into Sandra's office with its crisp human resources diploma and a picture of an uptight-looking woman who looked just like her, perm and all. I presumed it was her mother.

"I heard that I can now apply for health benefits … for my partner?"

"Excuse me, your who?"

"My partner. Sheelah." Sandra actually stood up from her chair on the other side of the desk while buttoning her beige crinoline blouse all the way to the top.

"I don't know about that. I haven't heard anything," Sandra said. Thankfully her assistant had entered the room by then.

"Jane, they are talking about it but we don't have anything in writing yet about how it will work. I'll call you as soon as I hear. It'll be a few weeks, I think," said Ina, smiling and touching my arm as she walked me out of Sandra's stiff office. "I think it's great that they are changing the benefits, by the way. How's your new puppy?"

"Great. Thanks, Ina. I appreciate it, everything."

⟨

Two years ago and approximately thirty years after I came out, a young woman came to speak to me after I'd read at the Pride Coffee House at Kootenay Pride in Nelson. She told me that even though the world is more accepting, it is very difficult to come out and my poems helped. She didn't feel she could come out to her religious community. She was twenty and suffering. It was a reminder that it still isn't easy. I felt grateful that my words had an impact and that she could talk to me, but I was surprised and saddened that people still struggle with coming out. I still go to Pride and not just to dance, though most of the town comes out and celebrates.

We used to have one protester at Pride in Nelson. He came wielding a Bible quotation on a placard, something about *abomination*. He was sort of a frumpy guy, usually with stained khakis and a long-sleeved plaid shirt, and stood on the corner of our main intersection. People used to laugh and be empathic to him. I wanted to tell him to go to hell, which says more about me than about him. His daughter came out to him a few years back and he's since stopped his one-man protest. Friends and allies line the streets to cheer on the queers.

In 2003 my triathlon training friend, Sally, remarked, "It's so supportive here. Do we need Pride in Nelson?"

"Ha! Good question. I'm not sure. I think we do, even if we are supported here. It's a solidarity thing with other parts of the world where it's not so easy." I chewed on this question for a decade. It inspired me to embark on what would become my second book of poems, *Acquired Community*. The book sought to answer these questions: How is our community resilient? How did we get from being hated to being tolerated and sometimes accepted? How did Pride marches shape and support me?

Pride was and still is a respite from shame as well as a reminder that our hard-won equal rights need to be defended. They can be so easily taken away, as we are seeing south of the border. Pride celebration may be marred this year by the recent decision of our council to no longer allow the Pride banner to be hung on Baker Street or the Pride flag to fly at city hall. This decision seemingly reduces the city's chance of litigation from the right-to-life crowd, who also have a banner that hangs on Baker Street for a week a year. There has been strong opposition to the anti-choice banner because its attempted shaming of women who are considering or have abortions is widely seen as different from celebrating and publicizing an event being held by a marginalized group, as the Pride banner does. That a progressive city such as Nelson should find itself refusing to publicly support a group that has been and still is marginalized, that continues to see victims of hate crimes at a much greater proportion than the heterosexual population and that is supposed to be protected under the Canadian Charter of Rights and Freedoms is a sad statement about the resurgence of populist extremism. If we have lulled ourselves into thinking of Nelson as uniformly supportive or at least laid back, live and let live, this is a cold-water splash to wake us up to the need to engage and hold our leaders to account.

A Different Path

Until the kids were eight years old, I worked full-time as a vocational rehabilitation consultant at WorkSafeBC, the provincial workers' compensation board. There, I worked with the most severely disabled/injured workers who could not return to their pre-injury jobs. It was, in many ways, rewarding work. Caseloads were sometimes high, there was not enough opportunity to meet with clients in person and the legislation pendulum had swung in favour of employers because of the politics of the day.

When we were more willing to acknowledge our children's needs, I requested part-time work because we believed that the kids really needed a parent with them after school every day, a safe container for their stress releases, a solid grounding at home. I tried to accomplish part-time work via job sharing but my employer denied this request because my fellow job sharer and I were not in the same physical location and this was not a precedent the company was willing to entertain. When I reluctantly explained to my union that I had two special-needs kids and could work only part-time, they fought for me but the employer wanted medical documentation to support this. I understood their need for this; the irony of how many times I had requested the same information from employees with disabilities was not lost on me. However, I found myself unwilling to provide very personal and private information to my human resources adviser about my children and their trauma. Perhaps I was unwilling to have them labelled by a new health professional, and knowing the system well enough, I realized it wouldn't mean just a trip to our family doctor, but multiple visits to a child psychologist specializing in adoption trauma. I wasn't willing to drag the twins around to specialists who would test them. If it had been just me, yes, I would have provided my medical information but this was a different story. Even if I was willing to put my kids through this, I was doubtful that a professional would agree to a medical accommodation of a parent working part-time in order to be home with children instead of having them cared for by competent paid caregivers, given our societal norms. Why was it imperative that it be us and not a skilled, paid caregiver? Call it parental intuition but I just knew fiercely that us being home and available for our kids after school was important in their attachment and hence their development, as was giving them days off now and then to calm their overtaxed systems down. Perhaps it was my endless quest to make up for lost connection time because we weren't there for their first fourteen months.

I didn't have the energy to put into that fight. I was so focused on my kids and their well-being. I also had hesitations about the work; one of the things that weighed on me most about my years at WorkSafeBC was what I see as a crisis of empathy. I understood this much more acutely after I sustained a workplace injury myself and had a claim with WorkSafeBC after a nasty fall in an icy parking lot while on a road trip in Cranbrook. My whiplash and concussion didn't heal well because it was diagnosed as only whiplash. The concussion was missed so it went untreated, which prolonged my recovery. I had so much dizziness and nausea, I actually wrote a poem about making dinner in five-minute intervals. It would take me all day. I walked for ten minutes at a time before my dizziness and muscle spasms kicked in. I eventually returned to work very gradually and lived with almost unbearable symptoms, all of which get labelled as "chronic pain" if one is not recovering within the time frames laid out in the insurance system. I was given a small chronic-pain payout in recognition of my not being healed when I was told to get back to work. It was a very difficult time. The medical advisers, doctors who review the incoming medical reports from treating practitioners, are never in contact with the claimants. I think this serves to protect them from their own empathy impacting "objective decisions." Fortunately, I eventually healed but it certainly wasn't within the expected timelines. Because of the number of people who try to game the system, the system is set up to minimize costs around claim times. The collateral damage is people who actually are not malingering but have functional impairments that are real but not explained by their diagnosis, either because of a knowledge gap about a particular diagnosis or because of a missed diagnosis.

There are individual case managers and vocational rehabilitation consultants with empathy who work in that system but it is not sought out in hiring nor rewarded in performance reviews. In fact, it is cautiously tolerated, with newly hired case managers being told they need to manage their empathetic tendencies in order to get the job done. Unfortunately, I saw a handful of power-hungry staff ride roughshod over their clients. This, when the clients are usually at the most vulnerable moments of their life: unable to work, diminished in their ability to do many things that give life satisfaction, uncertain about their futures. Typically these were staff who did not have a social work, social sciences or health sciences degree. Perhaps this is my bias and it could have been people who were burnt out from working in the system too long. I had one colleague boast that she had absolutely no empathy. Thankfully it was only a small handful who leaned away from empathy. That this icy efficiency was tolerated in the system at all wore me down. I am not a bleeding heart and there were times in my practice I had to take the tough-love approach. However, I found myself less willing to work in a system that rewarded reduced claim duration over most other outcomes. The curse of a creative, to be sensitive, I guess.

On any given day you may hear my reason for leaving WorkSafeBC as one of the above. You may also hear me talk about working part-time being a much better way for me to balance my job and my writing practice. The truth is multi-factored. Despite my reluctance to embrace this reality when it comes to the hardest experiences of my life, I do acknowledge its resonance: there is more than one truth. To my relief, the sky doesn't fall knowing this. My children are good teachers in this respect.

My energy was to be better spent elsewhere. I ultimately resigned from WorkSafeBC just after I returned to work full-time following my workplace injury. My resignation letter to WorkSafeBC was a poem I'd written entitled "Skunk Cabbage":

> I wasn't thinking of quitting my job on this morning walk,
> but the plant has convinced me,
> the logic of paycheque and pension is overrated.
> Art, too, can be this brash, nonsensical—
> plant that smells like an animal and is named for food.

I can only imagine what my manager thought. Turned out she was good humoured about it when she read it and as far as I could tell Work-SafeBC was sad to lose a valued, if non-conforming, employee, though not sad enough to change the system to allow for part-time employment. I don't begrudge them. They are just part of a system that behaves as if families still had one parent at home doing all the laundry, meal preparation, child nurturing, bill payments, gardening, house maintenance and other tasks that most families now must moonlight to complete. And this doesn't even account for families who have children with special needs or are taking care of an aging or ill parent. We need solutions at the government policy level that allow people to work part-time, their hours matched to the school day, without medicalizing the reason for the request of part-time work. I left Work-SafeBC and now own a consulting business in the same field. I have a shitty benefits package but a very good life. It's amazing how many fewer massage treatments you need when you have more job satisfaction and flexibility. The reduced hours don't hurt either.

Adoption leads me on a different path. I likely wouldn't have left WorkSafeBC had we not adopted kids but I am happier for it. I had worried that having kids would impact my writing but it has enriched it by far. I was concerned over the lack of quiet space and time but this has led me to prioritize and not squander the quiet time I have.

I KNOW WHAT HE DID

After Christmas dinner 2003, my father and I were looking after my niece, Ella, who would have been three at the time. In the midst of playing with her, she got a little wild and started flinging DVDs around the basement rec room.

"Ella, you can't do that, honey. Please stop."

My father chimed in, "Ella, you've got to stop throwing things."

"Nooooo," she screamed. She continued to escalate; DVDs landed all around us.

"Ella, I'm going to give you a little time to calm down." I sat her down, off to the side of the room but where she could see us, to break the near-tantrum spin she seemed to be in.

My brother James came stomping down the stairs, and seeing that his daughter was sitting apart from us on a time out, he lunged at me, screaming, "Fucking dyke, stay away from my kid. I'll fucking kill you."

"James, stop. You have to stop!" my father yelled. Ella was yelling something incoherent from across the room and throwing things again. I froze out of fear that I would be physically beaten or worse. My father's pleas finally jolted my brother and he backed away and stomped up the stairs, but not before grabbing his daughter. "Come on, Ella," he said.

My father and I sat among the ruins: my shocked system, my father's horror, a mess of Monty Python and various other DVDs. Although I didn't feel safe, knowing my brother was in the house, I felt witnessed and validated by my father and we stayed in the rec room talking for what seemed like a long time.

"Are you okay?" my dad asked gently. He was crying and shaking his head in disbelief. "I'm sorry this happened, Jane."

"I'm sorry too. What a fucking asshole," I said.

"He can't behave like this."

"He's always been an asshole."

"I'm kicking him out. I don't care if his house is not ready to move into, he can't stay here," my father stated. James, his wife and his daughter were living with my parents in their modest townhouse while their own house was being built.

My brother had spent the aftermath upstairs talking to my mother. I can only guess at the nature of the conversation, knowing what came next. I walked up the stairs and was greeted by glares from my mother. The dish rack was full of pots but the remnants of turkey dinner still occupied most available surfaces in their small kitchen, where my mother had been cleaning up after cooking the meal. "Get out!" she yelled.

"Who, me? You want *me* to get out? You must be joking." Though I was shaken by my brother's behaviour, my mother, who had witnessed nothing, yelling at and blaming me for the incident stunned me. After this futile exchange, and while my brother now lounged in the living room, I retreated to the cozy basement rec room built by my dad. "I'm leaving," I told him. "I don't feel safe here." I feared the footsteps I could hear from above would bear down on me, crushing my belief in the world.

"Yeah, I understand. I'll get this sorted with your mom."

I called my friends who lived forty-five minutes away and asked if they had a spare bed. While driving to their house, my need to connect with my new girlfriend grew deeper than my reluctance and shame at the incident. I called Amy. "My brother lashed out at me. I left."

"What? Oh God. Are you okay?"

"Yeah, but no."

"How did this happen? Are you still there?"

"No. I'm driving to Jo and Karen's house. I will be okay. James is a lunatic. Thankfully my dad was there."

"Are you sure you're okay? Will you call me when you get there? Can I call you back in a little while? My uncles and aunts are just leaving our house and I won't see them again before I leave St. Louis. I'm sorry. I wish I was there to wrap my arms around you."

I drove the rest of the dark, two-lane highway talking to myself, trying to process what the hell had just happened. I landed on my friends' doorstep teary eyed and in shock at nine thirty on Christmas night. My friends were outraged and supportive—reasonable voices in the sea of family crazy. We all, unfortunately, had more-than-average family dysfunction in common. I remember being grateful for chosen family as I sat safely by the wood stove of their peaceful home, trying to calm myself down enough to get some sleep. My fear that Amy would walk away from my baggage and me was unfounded, I learned after a phone call from her that lasted late into the night.

I still don't know why I didn't take further action. Perhaps it was disbelief that institutions, with their systemic homophobia, would help me. Perhaps it was, in part, the humiliation of having a brother of whom I was afraid. What kind of family raises someone capable of that? I wondered. Perhaps it was enough that my father had witnessed and validated the incident. At the time, I was under the mistaken belief that this would translate into some kind of fairness, that my brother would be reprimanded for his actions. Instead things took a turn for the worse after James threatened to cut my parents off from their grandchild. The threat was in reaction to my father saying he'd kick them out. My dad backed down.

I was in such shock, the injustice that I had already felt from other incidents deepened. For a long time I held on to the notion that if I'd only solicited outside help, then my mother would have to face facts and believe me. But now I see the folly in that. It is my opinion that I would have been blamed for ruining his life had I gone public. If my mother wasn't going to believe my father's version of events and was blind to his horror, then no one would convince her.

I'd already had my brother charged some years ago when he took a crowbar to my friend's truck, which was parked outside my parents' house. My queer friends and I arrived home from dinner to see it smashed to bits. My parents were away. I called the police. After my parents returned they talked to James. All I recall them saying to me was "Why did you have to call the police? Why didn't you just let him fix the truck? He has friends in the autobody business who could have done this for much less." I was incensed and stormed out. My brother served time on weekends and paid retribution. I didn't ever tell my parents about the other times he'd screamed "fucking dyke" at me.

It was hard to come to terms with the aftermath of my brother's behaviour. I wanted nothing to do with him unless he acknowledged what he had done and apologized. My boundary with James was not well received by my parents. They somehow thought I was asking them to take sides.

Things did not get better between my parents and me for a long time. Amy and I simply stayed away and asked that my parents visit us in Toronto, rather than us going to Kingston. Eventually we visited my mom and dad with our young twins. It was a huge undertaking to fly across the country with twin toddlers. On this visit, my brother showed up while my parents were out. He walked into the living room where I sat. I simply got up and walked out. His presence seemed aimed at merely pissing in the corners of our visit to my parents' home. Nevertheless, I was afraid and refused to expose my toddlers to any potential situations. I went for a walk around the neighbourhood rather than risk a confrontation. When my parents returned from their errand I said, "James showed up. I asked you to respect my boundary and I thought you agreed. Did you ask him not to come around while we were here?"

My mother yelled, "He's our son. He's the only child of ours that lives here. I'm not asking him to stay away."

"We are out of here. I can't believe this," I said, shaking my head.

I ran outside to the front lawn and heard my father and Amy having words. "What do you mean, he did nothing wrong on that Christmas night? What do you mean, you don't remember? Is that a joke?" Amy said.

I said through my tears, "Amy, we are packing up and getting out of here."

"Yeah, great idea."

Back inside we hastily crammed our clothes and toddler gear into our suitcases, forgetting the twins' blankies that they comforted themselves with before sleep. We left in a hurry, toddlers in arms, after this cringe-worthy shouting match on their front lawn. Amy yelled at my mom, "You are in denial. Wake up."

She yelled back, "You are tearing this family apart. Get over it." I was in disbelief and felt like crumpling to the ground.

My father had seemingly suppressed the horror of my brother's actions, though in a telling moment on the well-tended suburban lawn, he had yelled, "We can't cut him off. We need him. He's the only child that stayed. He just shingled our roof." This last bit stung, knowing I was the one who was called on to shingle the roof when I lived at home.

I tried to remain calm in the rental car as we got farther away from the family craziness. Amy once again validated my need for boundaries. I slowly let the tears come once we were at a safe distance, barrelling down the 401 toward Toronto and once again toward good friends who would welcome us unconditionally. I was also angry about whatever possible impacts this would have on my children. I was glad, in that moment, that we lived across the country from my family.

My most important tool in my disability management work is empathy, meeting people's humanity with my own and listening without judgment. I am unable to extend more than a sliver of this to my brother because I can't get past the injustice of being blamed for tearing our family apart. Before this incident, my family of origin hobbled along. In its aftermath, we were clearly and openly ruptured.

Estrangement is such an interesting word. Made strange. Feeling indifference or alienation or hostility to someone you used to love, care about. I don't know if it's the apt word here, for I don't remember a time when I felt affection for my brother. Perhaps when I was five and he was first born. My biggest recollections of him are of his being a difficult child, taking up much of my parents' capacity, and there being conflict because of it. He was the kid who peed on a neighbour who was sitting on our doorstep visiting with my mother. The kid who, when all three siblings were left to do something simple like the dishes, just wouldn't help or contribute. "Fuck off," he told us. I resented how much conflict he brought to many interactions. He was probably fighting for his territory among two siblings who were close and were always labelled "good kids."

When we were young, I was going out to play with friends in the fields and he followed. I said, "Stop following me. Leave us alone." He didn't. I used his shoelaces to tie his legs to a fence post across the road from our house. "There, now you can't follow us." I then wandered through the field to meet my friends. This act is a source of shame for me. Although I was only a child as well, I shouldn't have done it. I can see how it was an attempt at setting a boundary after he ignored my words. I got suitably reprimanded.

My parents took James to a psychologist, which was extremely rare for that generation and for working-class people. I think the enduring lesson they took from that experience is that children are all unique and parenting strategies may look very different depending upon the child. I gleaned that my parents felt guilty afterwards because they somehow failed to meet James's needs. All of this somehow seemed to morph into unconditional support for my brother. But that is my perception and I was not privy to their conversations. I do know my mother has invoked loving all her children no matter what as some sort of defence when my brother has done something inappropriate. "We love you all no matter what. We've never turned him away," my mother frequently said. Holding my brother accountable for his actions seems to have been lost in this process, as far as I can tell. I was left feeling not seen and unprotected by my mother.

I may, one day, get to that mountaintop of forgiveness that may well feel liberating, but I am down in the valley and the sun often only gets in via dappled light. I hold an enormous tension between the compassion I can feel for many people and my inability to find any for my brother.

My aunt, who is close to James, has apparently gotten his side of the story. She urged me to forgive and forget. In 2014, when I was in Victoria for a writer's festival, she brought up the subject while we were sitting in her car. "Your brother says he didn't really hurt you. He says you were mean to him when you were kids."

I felt the heat rising through my neck and face. "Didn't hurt me? He is big and strong and he came at me raging. It scared the hell out of me. Had my father not been there, things could have turned out much differently. Childhood rivalries are different than an adult attacking you." So there it was, the false equivalency. "He's never taken responsibility for his actions. And you know what? If I had a relationship to salvage, I might try to work it out, but we were never close." The last time we discussed this issue, which was over email, I asked my aunt why the onus is on me to forgive. I asked her what responsibility she would have to a perpetrator who mugged her on the street. We have agreed to disagree but I know that underneath all of this it pains her that our family is ruptured.

I don't know how to forgive someone who takes no responsibility for such an act. I don't think I need to forgive. I tend to think, like Rabbi Danya Ruttenberg speaking on CBC's *Tapestry* about Judaism and forgiveness, "atonement is between people and their God; forgiveness is not an obligation of the victim and really should only be asked for after making amends in a real way, after the perpetrator does the difficult work of repentance and goes directly to the person and asks for forgiveness."

I also like the Jewish saying "The gates of repentance are always open." I would add that the gates of forgiveness are open as well but not without repentance. Do I need to forgive myself for not forgiving? Perhaps, but I feel my unfinished business is only with my mother. I certainly need to practise letting go of expectations that my mother will "come around" and see this incident for what it was. At least she's mostly accepted my need for boundaries without expecting me to change. It's a work in progress. It takes a lot of practice.

On a writing retreat in Banff, I found myself angry all over again about this situation as I dove deep into writing about it. I took advantage of the very skilled psychologist made available to Banff Centre artists. She said that as people age they get more, not less, fixed in their beliefs. She helped me reflect on how my parents were unlikely to come around or see things from my perspective if they hadn't already in the time that had passed since the incident. It felt heartbreaking that after so much forgiveness between my mother and me and forging of a hard-won connection, we found ourselves here. It feels like my mother's denial is all shame driven, but that is my perception and not based on any conversations I've actually had with my mother.

It was an unbidden reckoning, then, that my father brought up my estrangement from my brother again during our last visit. He was very ill, in hospital and making amends before he died, as we both knew he soon would. In a blue hospital gown, from his wheelchair in a sunny corner lounge of a general floor of the hospital that seemed to house lost causes and the chronically ill, he said, "Your mother is upset that you and your brother don't get along." The clang of lunch dishes and alarms from expiring IVs faded as I listened and thought about my response. I looked at this old man before me with the blue-grey eyes, the whiskered face that seemed hollow after days of an ice-chip-only diet while they tried to sort out his diagnosis. Without his teeth in, he reminded me of the whiskered cadavers in anatomy class. They were housed in the basement of the Optometry building at the University of Waterloo. Our kinesiology class trudged there at eight thirty three mornings a week for our anatomy lab lesson. As I sat holding my dad's hand in the hospital, I tempered my initial desire to say, *What the fuck?*

I said gently, "Yes, I know that is very hard. It won't change unless he acknowledges what he did and apologizes."

"I know what he did." I examined his face, felt a flood of validation. "I remember. I understand why you don't want anything to do with him."

I saw the strain on my father's face, as if it took a lot out of him to *forget* that incident for so long. I feel forever grateful for this reckoning, both because it validates the experience that we shared, however horrible, and because, in my darkest times, I feel less alone. This was a remarkable moment of seeing and unseeing in my life. My father, after years of not seeing, saw.

As my youngest brother, Justin, says, parents protect the weakest child. This is his succinct explanation for my parents' hard-to-defend position. It feels like, on this issue, my mother has thrown me to the wolves. Fortunately for me, I long ago learned to live with the wolves and have learned to fend them off myself. Still, it feels very hard to sit with. I work around this incongruence in my story and focus on what a loving grandmother my mother is. She calls my son to talk hockey, specifically whether the Toronto Maple Leafs have won or squandered a lead the night before. It's a connection over three generations now, though some may say being a Leafs fan is a cross to bear. She talks fashion and pop culture with my daughter.

It drives a wedge in our hard-earned connection. I'm quietly devastated that this remains unresolved, that I have done what I can to foster a closer connection but that it remains limited and damaged. I'm uneasy that I can't write the rest of the story, that it is up to my mother to write. Perhaps it is even more incongruent to my mother and she too must sit with that discomfort. At times when we disagree, or when frustration surfaces, I seem to be judged on two things: that I live a long way from my mother and that I refuse any contact with my brother, though since their apparent falling out, this has waned.

My mother occasionally brings up my estranged brother. It seems like an ongoing attempt to humanize him. There have also been times I've listened to her rants about said brother. I tell her I don't want to hear the good or the bad, don't want to know about his life, but generally wish him well. Do I really wish him well? I wish he'd take responsibility for his actions but I no longer expect this. I am, gratefully, out of his life, except for minute interactions that I endured when my father was gravely ill. I will probably have to endure more when my mother is dying, especially if, like my father's, hers is a slow death. If my brother were to do the hard work of making amends and acknowledging the damage he has perpetrated, I would be open to a conversation. It's an interesting line between letting go and writing off. Normally, I am uncomfortable writing people off in my life. I encourage my kids not to do so, to see bad choices, not bad people, and to give people the benefit of the doubt. As a mother I now understand how painful it could be to have two of your children estranged from each other. Although my mother and I have come to some unspoken agreement not to talk about this, our relationship feels tentative. If I raised the issue, my mother might well tell me to fuck off.

I am aware that women are expected to carry out the role of keeping family together and that publicly speaking out about family violence is a betrayal of that ancient expectation. It is within this context that I come as close to understanding my shunning as I am able to at this point. It is

tribalism at its worst. I bring shame upon my family for naming unaccept-
able behaviour, for refusing to get along with my brother and perhaps most
of all for not going along with their collective denial. An obviously fractured
family brings the most shame. My parents' shunning of me seems to scream
How dare you betray our secrets to the world?

Remember that *Peanuts* cartoon? Snoopy on his doghouse clinking
glasses with Woodstock; "Love thy neighbor" is the caption. My *neighbour*,
in this case, my brother, is such a damn jerk. I have failed Charles Schulz. I
know this will not offer self-liberation, that I am not making many friends
in some faith communities with this stance. I am just not there, though I
have done much letting go. I focus on my own family and maintain a healthy
and loving connection with my youngest brother, Justin, despite the distance
between Thailand and Canada. I want nothing to do with James. I am okay
with that. However, now, as a parent, I have compassion for my mother's
sense of loss.

Love is easier when it doesn't involve actual people you know, to love
the world is easier than loving your brother.

OF QUIET DESPERATION

"Most men lead lives of quiet desperation" is a quote my father said often enough, not daily or weekly but when the opportunity presented itself. I never asked him why he quoted Henry David Thoreau; now it's too late. I know enough to know why. I don't think he fulfilled his dreams, squashed as he was by the class system. He never considered himself part of most men, though in this respect, I think he did, ever so quietly.

I feel that desperation sometimes as a woman. Sitting in my cubicle in Toronto, back in the day, working for the man, or in my case the mayor. Another day not writing. My job was varied and interesting but I found myself wanting more risk, more excitement. I considered going into the fire service after working with firefighters in safety and ergonomics. I was mesmerized by my shifts with firefighters during which I was to observe the physical demands of their job. On the night shift, I stayed at the fire hall, had a bunk and slept in my clothes with my stomach churning after eating a carnivore's dream dinner with the firefighters. They made us pasta and meat sauce and then another buff firefighter appeared with a stack of grilled sausages that flopped over the meat sauce on my plate. At the time I was a vegetarian. I couldn't come out to them, both because of the length they went to prepare dinner and because I was really trying to fit in, so I ate it all. We were out on calls steady through until about 2:30 a.m., then it went quiet until about 5:30 a.m.—three hours of sleep in the busiest fire hall in Canada on Adelaide Street in downtown Toronto.

I loved the sound of the alarm in the hall, even if it meant I had to get up in the middle of the night. I ran toward what I thought were the stairs only to realize, almost too late, that I was following one of the other guys on my crew and he was about to slide down the pole. I stopped myself by stretching a hand toward the pole. He was laughing by the time I met him at the bottom of the stairs beside the truck, trying to don the borrowed, ill-fitting bunker gear. There is something so extraordinary about riding through the darkened streets, almost devoid of traffic, the truck too heavy to smoothly recover from potholes. You have to contract your abdominal muscles to prevent your lumbar discs from bulging in these rigs.

We screeched to a halt at a fire call in the west end, on the fifth floor of a grim rent-geared-to-income building in South Parkdale. This neighbourhood is where all the people who used to live at the Queen Street mental health centre were discharged to when the government deinstitutionalized residents and patients en masse. They live alongside new immigrants. I wasn't allowed to go up to the actual fire until it was out and secured. On top of the grease-laden, old electric stove sat a charred pot and all of it was covered in foam with an inch of water on the floor. From this depressing apartment, the acrid smell of smoke and poverty rose.

Just as we were on our way back to the station, we got another call to an ugly scar of a building in South Parkdale. Bedraggled occupants stood outside. Some didn't bother leaving their units and instead watched from their windows, for there were no balconies on this basic complex. The firefighters shut off the false alarm, clanging in the night, after identifying the source. "They get tripped by cockroaches," said one of the firefighters I was on crew with.

To complete the observations for the job demands analysis; I was on call for any large fires and for salvage calls for weeks. Salvage is done after the fire is under control and when the building needs to be stabilized. There's a lot of overhead work, using pike poles to pull down smouldering or waterlogged drywall ceilings. The firefighters use shovels to remove burnt debris, with a few of them still operating the hoses to keep the smoulder down. It is macho work, even in the aftermath of a fire. It felt like their calls salvaged me from the despair of writing reports at my desk. I liked the thought of going toward a burning building when most sane people are running away from it. Something in me wanted to be a hero instead of a paper-pusher. There weren't many opportunities for women to be heroes. Maybe I wanted to be the one rescuing damsels in distress!

The Burn House is a test environment at the fire-training centre that heats up to a thousand degrees and has flames. I was invited to try it out after spending multiple shifts with the crews and expressing interest in applying to become a recruit. I donned the bunker gear and breathing apparatus. I loved the feeling of being in extreme, drop-dead heat and not getting burned. The danger, the potential that one mistake could cost your life, yet I walked out warm but safe. I loved it. I could have easily gotten hooked.

I went out for coffee with a group of female firefighters to decide if I was going to apply and put myself through the physically and mentally gruelling training. The adrenalin rush appealed. It held an allure I can't even explain but I did think it would move me farther from the *quiet desperation* I felt too. As far as I unpacked it, the desperation arose from needing more adrenalin than I had, from working through some deep emotional trauma and needing a job that forced me to immerse myself fully. That is, until I heard about the relentless sexism on the job.

"I can handle centrefolds in their lockers but don't appreciate finding them in my locker," one of the women said.

"Yeah, it was tough as a rookie. The guys didn't want to pair up with me. Said I got hired because I'm a woman. Said they doubted I could pull them out of a situation," another woman piped in.

"You still have to deal with that shit?" I asked.

"It's not that bad anymore. I've learned to tune it out and deal with it. We have a lot of great guys we work with as well."

But I could see the toll it took. Besides, I reasoned, I was in my mid-thirties by then; I was practically aged out, as most had joined in their early twenties. I knew then that I could not go backwards into sexist attitudes. I felt my own quiet desperation after this meeting. I knew that men had more opportunity and I modelled myself after them. Perhaps it was the sexism or the thought of stepping back in terms of money and not using my hard-earned post-secondary education that stopped me from pursuing the firefighting dream. I'm still happy to do ergonomics projects with firefighters once in a while. I'm happy, too, that shift work is a novelty and not a routine, knowing from my research that it wreaks havoc on people's bodies. And, I still have fun stories to tell my kids.

The sexism in the fire service reminded me of growing up amid my parents' and my brother James's attitudes. As much as I appreciated my father, he believed that women shouldn't learn to do woodworking, despite my obvious interest. He tried to teach my youngest brother, who had no interest at all.

It was a source of deep pride when my father asked me to help reshingle the roof of our house in Kingston. I was nineteen and fit. Still, it was hard work lugging heavy boxes of shingles on the roof via a ten-foot ladder. There was no such thing as a fall-arrest system in his tool box. We just leaned in toward the roof and away from the pavement as we hammered away in the hot sun. I had something to prove, that women could work hard and do "men's work."

Almost three decades later, in the adoption process, when it was down to three families being considered to adopt the twins, we were asked to write an essay on how we would ensure good male role models, especially for the boy we eventually came to know as Theo. Even the social workers thought that boys needed dads. In the absence of a dad, they wanted assurances that our children would have positive male influences in their lives. They seemed to assume that as a lesbian couple we didn't have any deep or lasting connections with men. This prompted an ongoing joke with our male friends about their having to try out to be positive role models for our kids. Often they come bearing masculine gifts, such as a bobble-head Thor, a football, and many toy trucks and tractors, vying for the honour.

Because we didn't see having a child as our biological right, that is, something that would just happen privately in the bedroom, a sperm's rightful swim to fertilize the egg, we rose to the occasion without getting too caught up on the intrusiveness of the adoption process. If this prize was going to be won by essay competition, then the English-lit major and the professional poet were going to give it their all, dammit. As we weren't given much time to write this, we met in a café over my lunch hour and banged out an articulate, compelling epistle. We assured the committee that we had lots of male friends, many of them dads, that the kids would have uncles involved and that, no, we were not the lesbian separatists they feared.

When he was ten, Theo played Atom hockey. He had good coaches. He loved the macho energy, the AC/DC in the dressing room, the buddy punches. He loves telling jokes and he had an appreciative audience. I was quietly proud that the boy with the lesbian moms could fit in. He was not at the top of the hierarchy that was reserved for the hockey stars, but he was and still is well liked.

I feel guilt and relief, too, that he's opting not to play organized hockey this year. Relief that I don't have to make small talk in the frozen arena stands. Though I passed, it took energy not to talk about sexism or the competitiveness that seems to permeate too soon into kids' hockey. The equal-play rule always got thrown out in the last few minutes of a close game. The most competitive players didn't pass to the one female player.

I felt less stressed knowing that early-morning long winter drives would be a thing of the past, for even Atom-league games were as far away as three hours' drive one way from Nelson. I felt relief also that my boy, small by North American standards, was not going to get creamed into the boards or checked when the game turns to a blood sport at around age fourteen. There was relief that I wouldn't feel the pressure to conform and not point out things I thought were off about traditions. When my son got the Soldier Award at the end of a game for hard work, he donned an army helmet. I was uncomfortable with militarization of the game but I would have been the freak had I pointed this out. Quiet desperation indeed.

It's complicated. I feel guilty that I wasn't gung-ho enough to push back when he said he might not play. Amy and I hold ourselves to some weird higher standard, as if we are on display. As a transracial, lesbian adoptive family, we often are. Internalized homophobia is with us in this way, ensuring we excel and are beyond reproach from the haters.

In grade one, Theo came home from school and said he wished he had a dad. When I asked him why, he said "because dads give piggybacks." Cue the piggyback rides for days in a row. Cue the horseplay. We can't be dads but we can sure as sugar give piggyback rides. Sure, we don't do stereotypically male activities such as hunt or high-mark on snowmobiles, but something tells me Theo will be fine without those skills. He sometimes needs jock rock and the testosterone surge but he gets that in the hockey dressing room or the baseball dugout with his lads and the coaches. He also gets it with family friends. Contrary to the popular myth, some of our best friends are straight men and inexplicably they ask us for advice on protective cup purchases for sports. Perhaps we are less threatening to ask than their male friends. This year my son is playing basketball. I am his coach. I first sought his permission. I wanted him to have the opportunity to say no and have a male coach instead.

Amy and I can both relate to our son in many ways. With our plaid shirts, jeans and comfortable shoes, it is more challenging to relate to our daughter's love of high heels, makeup and shopping. Thankfully Franny also plays soccer competitively and doesn't hold back in trying to conform to some unrealistic expectation that girls aren't supposed to be fierce. Decorum gets flung away when she is busy being a kid and chasing her brother or jumping on the trampoline.

My twins are many things I am not, including gender conforming. My daughter is a shopper. We can't and don't influence these things, except to open doors and provide encouragement. When my daughter was nine, she started saying "I hate gay couples" when she wanted to pick a fight. Perhaps she will look to some of those gay couples for fashion mentorship since she gets none at home.

Franny goes thrift-store shopping with Nana when we get together, which is usually a couple of times a year. She returns with dress-up clothes: high heels and sparkly sweaters and a deep love that comes with having that side of her seen and celebrated. At the same time Theo rides on Papa's tractor or they build something together.

As a family, we are strangely liberated from gender roles and find our own way. It is a satisfying journey even if we have extra explaining to do sometimes. I wouldn't trade it for the well-trodden path of expectations down which our straight friends tread. We don't have the chronic complaints of many of our heterosexual female friends that they still do the great bulk of the housework and child rearing, a reality that still fills me with quiet desperation. Fortunately, we walk our own path. We write our own stories.

IF YOU HAVE A BELLY BUTTON

From eleven to thirteen years old, I delivered the *Kingston Whig-Standard*. The paper route was over a large rural area, three to five kilometres, and I delivered only eighteen to twenty-two papers a day. Back then, before electronic payment options, carriers collected cash or cheques once a week from customers. A family called the Sweets signed up on some sort of promotional deal and continued receiving the paper without having to pay for a while. Eventually, I was expected to collect a fee for the previous weeks and so instead of tossing the plastic-wrapped paper at their weathered and damaged doorstep on a damp March day, I knocked. Mr. Sweet opened the door of their worn insulbrick house and the stench of body odour and stale cigarette smoke greeted me. Across the dirt floor, Mrs. Sweet sat at the kitchen table drinking from a brown stubby in a blue haze of cigarette smoke. I went to school with their children, whom we all teased relentlessly about their smell, their dirty clothes and their inadequate or absent lunches.

"You owe me money for the paper," I tentatively said.

"Next week," Mr. Sweet said.

I returned the next week. The walk to their door seemed long. I knocked quietly. "Remember? The paper? You owe me four dollars," I said reluctantly.

"I don't owe you no goddamned four dollars. Get out. Get the hell out!" Mr. Sweet grabbed his shotgun in one hand and held it, not waving it like a crazy person but keeping it close like an amulet. While he stood in his doorway, I ran off with my papers slung across one shoulder in their canvas bag. I sprinted through the thawing farmer's field to my other customers and finished my route, scared and confused.

That I didn't tell my parents right away is not surprising. Mr. Sweet and his shotgun led me to believe I'd done something wrong. His shame was presumably a combination of not being able to pay, his failure due to his poverty and his kids being teased and shunned. This was all packed in the barrel of that gun. I eventually called the newspaper and told the circulation manager what had happened. The manager's alarm served as a reality check for me of how inappropriate this customer had been. I was told never to go back there. I do not know if they called the police or how it all ended but the matter never came up again.

The next time I saw the Sweet kids, they were emptying their pockets of change at the counter of the Lucky Dollar convenience store in our neighbourhood. Although they were short, the store owner gave them the box of Kraft Dinner anyway. I felt badly for them.

Although I had always remembered factual details of my sexual violation, it was devoid of emotion. I had split off from feelings in order to survive. Eventually, feeling those raw, difficult emotions cascaded me into the depths of shame. Like the raging Mr. Sweet, I had a shotgun of shame but turned it toward myself. I simply was not ready to feel the associated powerlessness so I blamed myself. It was my fault because I went over to my perpetrator's house, albeit to see my friend, his youngest sister. It was my fault because initially I liked the attention. It was my fault because I returned to their house. It was my fault because if it was not, then I was completely at the mercy of a sociopath. Split off from that story and the accompanying emotions, I spent some counselling sessions doing psychodrama around this and physically expunging the sensation from my body.

"I feel like I'm choking and gagging. I've felt like this all week since our last session."

"What do you think is going on?" my therapist asked.

"I don't know. I wasn't violated that way. Not that I remember."

"Let's make some noise, see if we can get that feeling out." To passersby it must have sounded like an untalented singer warming up, guttural sounds emanating from my depths.

"How does that feel?" my therapist asked.

"I can swallow. I don't feel as nauseous. Better, I guess."

"Try and get it out like this for a few minutes every day."

It was gruesome work, coughing up terror. Daily, I felt despair. The thing about despair is that you feel as if you will never escape it. I do not wish this upon anyone, obviously, but I can say that I learned some things that may help me better parent my children. My therapist told me my critical voice was killing me. It was. The *I'm not good enough* soundtrack was piped into my brain at all hours.

To work on shame is to diminish but never to eradicate it. It is like the square root of a square root; the answer is never zero. On downward-spiralling days, I still question why I "allowed" my sexual violation to happen. Complicity is still easier than powerlessness. Mostly, though, I am able to stick with my new, hard-earned narrative, that I was in fact powerless, that as an eight- and nine-year-old, I was not at fault. The antidote to this shame was speaking about it, uncovering every dark corner in therapy. The initial incident pales in comparison with the isolation that shame enforced over my life for two decades.

I have felt run-of-the-mill shame too. What woman hasn't felt ambient shame in our culture? Body shame: my particular twist on this is not being feminine enough in addition to the usual, being too large. My antidote to this is to embrace my own unique fashion that is not a sellout for my body; frills are not for me. I tend toward androgynous clothes, boxy, oversized shirts, though I started wearing colourful scarves when I turned fifty. I am fit and curvy, I work out regularly and this, I tell myself, has to be enough to feel good about my body. It's a work in progress.

𝑒

Our family has dinner together most evenings. It is one of the most important parts of my day and I feel fiercely protective of and committed to this ritual. I have my mom to thank for that. We take turns cooking and if the kids aren't at sports or music practice, they help too. We play "peaches and pits," in which we each say something that we loved about our day and something that we didn't. "My peach is going mountain biking with Mama; my pit is doing chores" is a typical one from the kids. The kids delight in hearing that they were part of my peach. Often I do two peaches. Sometimes we are part of each other's pits too, which is hard but offers us a chance to reflect and change how we treat each other. My kids roll their eyes at having to play, but when a guest comes over they are the first to tell the visitor about the game. They made up a rule that if you don't have a pit, you get a wedgie. It sort of makes sense that you need to have something to not enjoy. Toughens you up perhaps. We don't enforce it with guests.

One of our favourite family sayings is "If you have a belly button, you can make mistakes." Thanks to the kids' grade-one teacher for that. We use this when we are talking about our respective days. It's a fun way to catch up with each other and I always make sure to let them know of my challenges and failures so they can give themselves permission to fail too. I became aware of this as I watched my children being so hard on themselves. Both barely give themselves time to learn before saying things like "I'm useless at this." Sometimes I think a big part of parenting is helping them to get over failure, failure they will inevitably have and must learn to not get overwhelmed by.

I hope that this sense of not being good enough has not come from us, their cheerleader parents, but I can see how hard we are on ourselves so perhaps it has, after all. I can also see that as older parents who have solid careers, we aren't failing on a daily basis. We've learned some things along the way and, on good days, I like to think I make fewer mistakes than I used to at work. I made sure I shared the biggest regret of my career as an ergonomist. I didn't ever apply for my professional certification because of a lack of confidence. I had imposter syndrome for a while. The certification was put in place many years after I finished school and I worried that I wouldn't be accredited. This became an ongoing source of shame and regret.

I also witness both of us working feverishly on creative projects. I haven't found a way to get around precision and attention to detail that ends up taking hours and hours, no matter how much one has done to prepare for a deadline. Hence, "I can't play with you; I'm trying to finish this poem." And the many discussions we've had about trying to get something "right." They watch all of this and perhaps by osmosis learn that we push ourselves hard and they must too.

Not long ago, I arrived home and realized I'd forgotten half of my groceries at a store an hour away. I was frustrated with myself. It became my pit during our round of peaches and pits at dinner. Theo pulled up my shirt to reveal my belly button and said, "You have a belly button!" Indeed.

Theo's beautiful response helped me later. "I'm hungry," he said tentatively. Usually I would feel frustrated and say, "But I just asked you if you were hungry before we came upstairs, before you brushed your teeth. You said no." This time I said, "Okay, honey. Let's get you some food. You must be growing again."

He visibly relaxed because I wasn't shaming him this time. "Thanks, Mom."

"You have a belly button too," I said as we made our way down to the quiet kitchen to get him a bowl of Cheerios. I felt sad that I had ever shamed him.

When my son was in grade five, a classmate uttered a racial slur at him. I am told that Theo just looked at the kid and said, "Seriously, you just said that?" Then he chuckled. Then my daughter stood up and told the kid off, as did a large handful of classmates. My son felt supported. I detected not a shred of shame at this attempted shaming from a peer. Though racism sucks, his peers couldn't have reacted better. If only the principal had been able to see this racist incident for what it was instead of being defensive. I never would have wished this upon him but the silver lining is the resilience he is building and the support he felt from peers. The other silver lining is that he and Franny told us about it, we were able to support them and it opened up a conversation about racism—a conversation that we need to keep having as they find their way in the world.

My hope is to provide alternatives to shame pathways in my children's brains. *I made a mistake* versus *I am a mistake.* (Thanks for that, Brené Brown.) My kids already have remnants of my legacy of shame. My hope is that this will also lead to empathy for themselves and hence others out in the world.

Though I don't pretend to know what lies ahead for my children on their respective journeys, I am determined to see them and let them know they are seen. I hope I can walk with them for a while. I hope with all my heart that they do not have to experience any Mr. Sweet moments. I don't want them to feel desperately alone like I did; I know shame flourishes in silence.

Shame, sadness, crisis, all are manifested when one's internal story doesn't match up with external reality. They must be reconciled, must be made whole so we can have a narrative of our lives that makes sense, that we can live with. On CBC's *The Enright Files*, Man Booker Prize–winning writer Anne Enright says all writing is shame management. Writing the stories of our lives and being our children's co-authors is a potent antidote.

How I Met My Wife

In 2003, when I took a seven-month leave from my Big Toronto Job, I moved to Nelson. This was my reward for graduating from years of emotional healing work. In Nelson, I wrote poetry, trained for triathlons, canoed, hiked and even learned to juggle after a few months of purposeful activity.

My mother grew weary and worried, said it was time to "get back to real life" after many weeks of blissed-out phone calls from me. I'd never felt so real: falling in love with a place and a community and falling in love from afar, through letters, with the woman I would eventually marry.

Just a few months before I left Toronto for my sabbatical, I met Amy on the basketball court. I was on the white team that dominated and she was on the red team that was losing every game. Though Rainbow Hoops was competitive, by its very nature, as a lesbian basketball league, it was also egalitarian and one team was not allowed to dominate. For some of the feminists among us, it would have been great if each game ended in a tie. Indeed, not keeping score would have been the ultimate, though you can't take competitive spirit out of women who had so often been shunned in other arenas, such as dating boys, and shone in athletic and academic competition. It was a melting pot for lesbian feminists and lesbian jocks. They equalized the teams a few games into the season and I was traded to Amy's. The advantage this afforded me was commensurate with that time of my life. I was coming out of the slumber of my long-term relationship and grabbing the world by its horns. I was fit and felt good in my skin and was labelled a skilled basketball player. Right away we clicked, passing the ball to each other, each knowing exactly where the other was positioned, as if we'd played together for years. If meeting my future wife in a sports league sounds like a lesbian cliché, it was.

For the first time, I believed that I deserved to be happy. I had just finished the deepest of my healing work with a psychotherapist. I was fresh out of a six-year relationship with Kate that, while nurturing, was not passionate and was twisting my gut with its truth. I had joint custody of a sweet golden lab, a great job and good friends and I was healthy.

In other words, it was time to get out of my comfort zone. Safety was not this hot woman on the basketball court because I cared too much about her already. I was taken; I had so lost my sense of objectivity that my friends humoured me and appeared at Rainbow Hoops on a Saturday night and confirmed my hunch. My friends were impressed but, more importantly, I was smitten and falling in love, though it would be months before I said that out loud through the safety of letters from Nelson. Come to think of it, those letters were anything but safe, all vulnerability and heart opening. The last few lines of my poem "Fever of Gratitude," in *Steeling Effects*, started as a musing in one of those love letters and illustrates the point:

> ... by day the grasses grow redder,
> in a fever of gratitude ...
> I want to rest like quiet blades of grass
> in each other's arms, alive and steaming.

Though she was the twenty-four-seven director of a large residential Y camp, Amy found time to make CDs chock full of lesbian anthems, odes to love and resilience, and sent them to me. I loved her willingness to take a chance on love and her spontaneity. She flew across the country and visited me for the May long weekend or, as her friend called it, Forest Fuckfest, in a bid to reassure her it could just be a fun weekend, not laden with deep expectation. I remember hiking up Fry Creek Canyon together from the alluvial fan that edged Kootenay Lake, where we camped. We were with two good friends from Nelson but frequently lingered alone for long kisses in the fragrant woods, the roar of Fry Creek in its May climax beside us. Occasionally submerged boulders could be heard shifting with the thrust of the waterfall. The boulders sounded like bone dominoes being shuffled in between games, but an octave or two lower.

The cliché that women deeply connect emotionally is true, at least for me. When we first got together we would leave the lights on in intimate moments to fully see each other. Days we lay entwined in her high-ceilinged bedroom at the back of her Cabbagetown flat, the small window barely noticed except for the extra light it brought so we could regard each other more closely. Occasionally we got up for food, but I quickly learned she was

no foodie and the cupboards were bare except for pasta shells with pow-
dered cheese, albeit organic, and cans of tuna. Once in a while we surfaced
for a grocery run, making pad Thai late on a Sunday night, stretching out
the weekend as far as we could. Predictably, we bagged on many plans with
friends, and sometimes on work. Our intimate world was what mattered,
getting to know every inch of each other, learning our histories, sharing experiences. I'd like to say it was all shooting stars, physically and spiritually,
but romantic silliness is not worthy: Side by side we burned ourselves out
light years away? Twinkling stars permanently a fixed distance from one another in the cold atmosphere? No, we were more earthly than that.

The first night I stayed over it snowed heavily; fat flakes in no hurry
somehow accumulated to twenty centimetres by morning. When I finally
left her house, only because she had a squash game booked, ironically enough
with her ex, I walked out into a city transformed, a wonderland: people helping dig out their cars together and children making snowmen in their post-
age-stamp front yards, the sound of cars and streetcars muffled. The city had
remade itself in a white dress that, despite knowing better, we thought of as
virginal. It seemed we all contracted to suspend our knowing that it would
melt into gritty grey underfoot. We kissed goodbye at the front door of her
house. I swept my forest-green car off and tried to drive away only to find
myself stuck in snow. Sheepishly I returned to her flat and asked her for help
digging out, but not before I had considered calling a tow truck instead, for
I was very reluctant to pepper the sacred with the mundane. If I was completely honest, I did not want to rely on her for help. Besides, I was a little
embarrassed that I had such an unsexy car, though deep down I was proud
that I had enough self-esteem to drive a Ford Focus wagon. She laughed and
helped me and we kissed shyly out in bright sun before I pulled away.

ℓ

My father had already met Amy at the culmination of our cross-country
trip together, in Toronto. We all had a beer together before we unceremoni-
ously dropped him off to take the night bus home to Kingston. I introduced
Amy to my mother on a weekend trip home later that fall. My family was
friendly, warm and welcoming, likely taking cues from my happiness. They
got along like gangbusters, my girlfriend understanding my mother better
than I ever could. They gossiped about movie stars and chuckled at my
obliviousness to popular culture. And Amy fell in love with my three-year-
old, very energetic niece, Ella, whom we took to the playground and for

walks. My British father didn't like the USA and was cautious about Americans, a remnant of his feelings about how they profited from World War II, took most of the credit and suffered fewer of the casualties than the rest of the Allies, but he seemed to genuinely like this American after spending the weekend together.

Amy's mother came from St. Louis for a weekend visit. She bought us dinner at a hip theatre-district bistro and we went to a Mirvish play at the Prince of Wales Theatre across the street from my office at Metro Hall in downtown Toronto. It was some forgettable musical, my first but not my last with my musical-loving in-laws. I remain less than a fan, though my wife does like to remind me that my favourite band is Queen. If you've ever watched them perform "Bohemian Rhapsody," you will know she has a point. Amy was delighted afterwards that my meeting the first of her family members had gone so well, but I didn't have a read on it, having failed to penetrate her mother's Midwest politeness other than her adoration of her daughter, and in that we had much common ground.

Months later, Amy and I drove from Toronto to St. Louis for her family's American Thanksgiving. When you enter Amy's stately family home through the garage, a nearly life-sized portrait of a young woman in a navy prom dress and kid gloves greets you. A debutante portrait, it turns out. My debutante, though I didn't even recognize her. Without any hints, I would have guessed it was a relative and one who was far less comfortable in her skin than I know my partner to be. I was speechless when I found out it was Amy. It was her equivalent of my mother offering to take care of my child should I have had one when I was a teenager: the pinnacle of projected dreams from our respective mothers. An unseeing of their daughters. I am told that the portrait was painted from a photo of Amy. The artist chose to leave out the enormous red blotches on Amy's neck, the result of anger and humiliation at having to participate in something she didn't believe in. Like pentimento, the blotches somehow left their mark, and the painting, which used to feature prominently in the myriad of portraits and framed photos hung in the living room, was quietly rehung in the hallway between garage and pantry where only family would ever see. It lingers like a beautifully crafted artifact of a terrible episode: a Winslow Homer painting from the American Civil War, but alas, I give the portrait painter too much credit.

This is the only time I've seen Amy in a dress. Other than the saying "Handle with kid gloves," I didn't have any clue that kid gloves were really a thing until Amy explained they were gloves made of very soft leather from goat kids, used for not leaving a trace and for showing off one's wealth. I also didn't know what a debutante was, England having evolved from this practice many decades before I came along and, truthfully, it never having been a tradition in my working-class background. As I learned about the custom, I was both incredulous and sad for her. The debutante ball, or Veiled Prophet Ball, as it was also known in St. Louis, is full of elaborate ritual. Elite peers anonymously choose the Veiled Prophet (VP), who then "presents" the young women to society to be scooped up by eligible bachelors. The VP chooses a Queen of Love and Beauty, with whom he dances a "royal quadrille" before presenting her with a tiara or pearls. My wife did not get chosen, nor was her father, merely an eye surgeon instead of a Monsanto owner, chosen to be the Veiled Prophet.

This was the world that her mother wanted for Amy. This was the world Amy begrudgingly entered when her mother pleaded, saying "It is the last thing I ask you to do." (It wasn't.)

In working-class families there is no equivalent, though once at a lesbian and gay barbecue in the Parkdale neighbourhood of Toronto, a Polish gay man marched right over to me with a solid-looking dyke, grabbed her breasts and said, "Nice strong woman. Nice tits. She wants you." There were no kid gloves and only the slightest pomp when I politely rejected her advances through her crass proxy.

A Cold and Broken Hallelujah

Our 2017 trip to Asia was conceived as a warm-up for our eventual goal of taking the kids to India, where their birth mother was born. We knew from friends that it could be confusing taking kids to India who look Indian but are not culturally Indian. We also knew that India would be a challenging place to travel for all kinds of reasons, such as poverty, pollution and population density, and we weren't yet up for it with nine-year-olds. We decided on Hanoi, Vietnam, instead. It was on the way home from Thailand, where we visited my brother Justin for two weeks, first on a beach vacation in the south and then in his home in Chiang Mai. We rationalized that while Hanoi may not be the most kid-friendly of destinations, at least the kids would have had a lot of kid-focused time already. My wife had visited twenty years prior and she wanted to see the Asian tiger emerged from the rubble of thirty years of war. This country that sent the Americans packing from what they called the American War and what we call the Vietnam War fascinated me. They had a government policy of "official forgetting" regarding their wars.

Unable to find a suitable hotel with a pool in old Hanoi, we ventured out to the Army Guest House Hotel for a swim. They had the only pool even close to old Hanoi and it felt as though the hotel was crumbling around the pool. The frigid pool with its too-deep shallow end provided only mild relief from whining and boredom at being dragged around to museums and markets. Vietnamese water puppet theatre was the most kid-friendly activity we found in the bustle and chaos of old Hanoi. Instead of a stage, there is a waist-deep pool and the lacquered wooden puppets move through the water in this otherwise conventional theatre space. The puppeteers control the puppets via rods from behind a bamboo screen, invisible to the audience. The orchestra plays traditional northern Vietnamese instruments from a balcony. The kids tolerated the story and even enjoyed it when they forgot about their policy of "official boredom." We decided to celebrate this small victory and take everyone out for a coffee and treat afterwards at an iconic westernized café that overlooked Hoan Kiem Lake. A little familiarity would be good after three weeks on the road, we reasoned. At the café, Franny demanded caffeinated coffee. "No. You know you aren't allowed coffee."

"I want coffee and I want two treats."

"You can have lemonade or an ice cream. You can have a lemon tart."

"Coffee!" she demanded like a spoiled toddler. We received our order, including an herbal tea for her, and found seats in the bustling café. "I hate this tea." She spat it back in the cup. "I want some new shoes on the way home. I want a necklace and a purse."

"That's a lot of things. Maybe we can look for one of those things in the market on the way, if you settle down."

She ran out of the café and we followed. She screamed, "You are the worst parents in the world. I hate you. You need to buy me a purse and shoes. Now."

I walked after her, so caught off guard that I tried to reason with her. "Franny, we will get you something but not when you behave like this. You know this behaviour gets you nowhere."

"I hate you!" she yelled and hit me as she ran off.

I ran after her in the crowded streets as dusk settled and people gathered round the Sunday night market full of food vendors, street performers and scooters whizzing through it all. "Franny, that's enough. You can't talk to us like this. You will get nothing."

She screamed more and I raised my voice too. "That's enough!"

Amy took over, consoling her calmly and then escalating too as Franny expertly pushed our buttons. The locals and tourists alike watched us perplexed, wondering whether we were the awful parents of her accusations, their contempt visible when we both raised our voices. We were both so mad we stormed back to our hotel, Theo in tow, all of us avoiding the crowds and scooters and Franny's attempts to hit and kick us. I asked myself *Why, why does she have to do this?* on the ten-minute walk back, along crooked foreign streets whose names I couldn't read.

In those moments I must admit I sometimes hope for a small injury to befall Franny. Nothing serious, and I have never made anything like that happen. Sometimes physical pain gives her permission to cry. When she is flailing around or lashing out, she has occasionally fallen or hit her arm on something and it temporarily stops the madness, a portal into sadness from the anger she is expressing. The extreme anger is an inoculation against sadness, it seems. It's like the tween equivalent to the inconsolable crying they did when they were little.

I do not know what makes our daughter want luxury and behave like she is entitled but my hunch is it is related to early loss and being out of control. Retail therapy at its best and most tragic. We call her Five-Star Franny under our breath, when she ramps up into this behaviour. It is difficult for this working-class woman to imagine, growing up as I did with a strong dose of *You are not special and don't take up space*. Entitlement is something I bristle at. I feel despair in these Givenchy moments. I ask myself what we have done wrong. I recognize that my daughter and I are probably at opposite ends of a spectrum. I swallow my disdain and try to lighten up, reasoning that retail therapy is ubiquitous and not the worst travesty. Franny is a fashionista. She would shop every weekend if we were so inclined. She laments that we don't live near a real shopping mall with Old Navy and Target. She has a collection of high-heeled boots. That she is allowed to wear them only for dress-up inside our house matters not. We joke that it skips a generation because both of her grandmothers are very happy to indulge her love of fashion, having missed out with their respective tomboy daughters. My mother may have gotten her "fix" dressing mannequins in her display-person role at work because she couldn't influence my fashion choices.

Back in our hotel, we lay on the beds exhausted. It turned out the rage was a precursor to grieving. As we approached bedtime, Franny was now sobbing over Leonard Cohen's death. She didn't know him. She knew the song "Hallelujah" and interestingly liked his gravelly version better than k.d. lang's version, which we frequently listened to. She sobbed about the death of "the man with the voice whose name I don't know." She described her heart as one side loss and one side love. She weighed her losses: her birth mom, her foster parents, her uncle Tom (actually my wife's uncle who had just died). The other side, love: her moms, her brother, her dog, her grandparents, her friends, her cousins, her uncles Justin and Youngmin. We cried too in the dark and she finally exhausted her tears, let us hold her and fell asleep. She lets us in, further in. This is her developing her own story, making sense of her story. "Hallelujah" indeed. The following is an excerpt from my poem of the same name:

The red bed spread sums my losses on one side,
my love on the other.
Why is the measure of love, loss?
And love is not a victory march,
It's a cold and it's a broken hallelujah.

Whichever one you heard, the holy or the broken,
both.
Praise in face of confusion.
Praise in face of broken or holy,
placeholder for reconciliation.

My father died last year. I had him for fifty-one years and my last words to him were "I love you." I still feel the loss and yet here was this nine-year-old making sense of her loss, writing her story. I like to think that at our best we are giving our twins opportunities to love, and to expand love, knowing loss is the other side of it—to love anyway. We have a lot of love in our home, lots of hugs, lots of connection; we tell our kids we love them every day. As in Mary Oliver's poem "In Blackwater Woods," *the black river of loss whose other side is salvation.* To love knowing there is this loss. Adopted kids often have the opportunity to learn this lesson much earlier than most.

I Married a Debutante

What does a lesbian take on a second date? Answer: *A U-Haul.* Unlike the joke, we didn't move in together until eighteen months after we met and even then it was as Amy was going off to live at the camp she directed for four months of the year. Over the Saturday *Globe and Mail,* I'd proposed living together. I hand wrote the question in the classifieds. Apartment for rent—*will you live with me?* I made the practical argument that we spend most nights together anyway and that we'd each save 50 percent of our current rent, but we both knew the real reason went beyond that and that we'd make the decision with our hearts. She moved into my flat, which we dubbed Stucco Palace, in June 2004. The walls looked like tidal waves, such that our heads would be jabbed with stucco if we attempted to recline while sitting on the couch. We celebrated the decision to move in together by eating roasted corn on the cob with lime and chilies from the street vendor around the corner in the ever-festive Little India neighbourhood at Gerrard and Coxwell. Though we didn't know it at the time, we were learning about the southern Indian culture that would play an important role in our future lives as parents.

Our flat came with a yapping, fierce Jack Russell that lived below on the first floor. It terrorized my very laid-back and friendly golden lab, Bella. Other than this pesky dog that broke our reverie each time we exited and entered, we blissed out, cohabitating and planning our escape from Toronto.

While Amy was away at camp, I typically visited her—twenty-four hours off every seven days didn't allow for much of a visit if she drove back to the sweltering city. Weekends in Muskoka sounded more idyllic than they are when your partner runs a summer camp with 350 kids on site and you stay in the director's cabin in the middle of it all. I remember being out for dinner together on the third hour of her twenty-four hours off and Amy getting a phone call saying a bunch of camp staff had been drinking. She had to return and, as dictated by the employee contracts, fire all the underage staff who had broken the rules.

Fortunately we also had use of the cabin in the winter when the camp was dormant. Weekends by the fire after a snowshoe or a ski across a frozen lake were an antidote to living in the city. Amy stamped out "Marry Me" in the deep snow, the letters thick as the width of her snowshoes. The letters were so large, I'm sure passing jets could have seen them. It was presented as a lighthearted joke but we both knew the depth of the love we were continuing to fall into. Her creepy facilities guy saw the "Marry Me" message when he was back on site and asked her about it. She feigned innocence.

Nevertheless we were wed two years later. It was both a political and a personal decision. I wanted to exercise my new right to get married. I wanted to honour all my brothers and sisters who had fought so hard for that right. I never thought this would be possible when I first came out. We wrote our own vows, my concluding line from which was "Above all, I will see you, with my eyes and my heart as open as I am able."

Our wedding announcement, September 17, 2005:

> We got married! Yesterday at noon at Toronto City Hall, we had an intimate ceremony with two friends as witnesses. We've been talking about this for some time but only decided to actually make a date on our 2nd year anniversary—Sept 6th. We decided it would be fun to do this before hopping on a plane to British Columbia, turning our two week vacation into our honeymoon. While the actual ceremony was spontaneous and informal, our commitment is lifelong and entered into with thoughtful care.
>
> While we are breaking the news after the fact to everyone, we would like to have a celebration with all of you sometime in the near future. We want to have you present to support our marriage. To us, marriage is about enriching and supporting each other through this life and an expression of how we want to be in the world—close and connected.
>
> What seems the most conventional of acts is a radical act for two women in love. We are proud to publicly declare our life long commitment and to exercise our newly

won rights as lesbians. We are saying yes to all the rights and responsibilities that go with it. We are proud to be married, in a country that has recognized gays and lesbians as equal under the law. We are doing this as a political as well as a personal act.

Thanks to each of you for believing in and supporting our relationship along the way. We look forward to celebrating this with you.

Love, Amy and Jane

Both of us were relieved to have only two friends there and not have to pull ourselves out of this sacred moment to interact with a horde of guests at a fancy reception. Even after being out for over ten years, Amy wanted to protect a sacred moment from the anticipated and unspoken disappointment and grief her mom would likely feel as she took the biggest step yet into this "alternative lifestyle." Unfortunately, my parents were collateral damage in that decision, for they would have loved to witness our wedding vows and would have been totally supportive. I could understand the vulnerability of not having a parent show up 100 percent during such an important moment. Also, it was an adventure to tell only two friends and to hop a plane. I think it also was an act, perhaps unconscious at the time, of us declaring that our life together belonged to us and no one else. We did not need our parents to see us in that moment. That said, Amy's parents have come a long way. When we did have a wedding celebration three years later with family and friends, her mother was very supportive and seemed genuinely happy for us, flowers in hand, speaking from the heart at our ceremony.

At the start of our honeymoon, all the way from Vancouver, we called and emailed our friends and family with our news. Amy came out and announced our wedding all in one email to her grandmother. Thankfully her progressive aunt was there to pick up the pieces. Her grandma did stare at me as if I had two heads at Thanksgiving dinner that year. Dinner was a rather formal affair compared with my family's Thanksgiving. I was even more conscious of the way I cut my smoked turkey, which fork I used, than I was the first time I visited. I'm quite sure I grabbed the wrong napkin, despite Amy having coached me in jest with lessons she'd learned from Pretty As a Picture, the charm school her mother insisted she attend as a young woman. It had taught my wife where to put the water glass and whom to serve first (the eldest female). I had no such advantage and probably bobbled my way through, which no doubt only reinforced what her mother already strongly suspected, that I was not from the same class. Now her grandmother had a few reasons to gawk.

On our dreamy BC honeymoon, after cycling north on the Sunshine Coast and south on Vancouver Island, with a few days' respite in Tofino, we drove to Nelson. We hiked up to Silver Spray Cabin, a steep, no-nonsense trail that was developed by miners to get to the silver ore. A forest fire had recently ravaged the trail, leaving the charred epithelium of trees, leafless with their blond, unburned inner layers, and much more light exposure than otherwise would be the case in this dense rain forest. Fireweed bloomed fuchsia among the black skeletons.

One of the magical things about hiking in the Kootenays is that once you get up above the dense foliage and into alpine views, you understand how in the middle of the mountains you really are. They stretch as far as the eye can see, in every direction, some of the higher ones with glaciers but most blue hued at dusk, a breathtaking silhouette of solitude. It was on the helipad of Silver Spray Cabin where my up-to-that-point-uncertain wife said, "Why wouldn't we want to live here? This could be our backyard. This is it." And so it was decided. We would figure out how to disentangle from our busy lives and emigrate from downtown Toronto to this wild place: this place of many immigrants who, over the generations, had sought their vocations in silver, in timber, in peace and now in creative reinvention.

I felt as if I was following in my parents' footsteps in some ways, moving to a very different place, more wild than the place we left. Though this was by choice, not economic necessity, both were decisions based on improving quality of life. Though my parents were sad about us moving away, they understood.

With mortgage secured, we went back east to resign from our jobs and pack up our lives. Moving rates were a dollar a pound so we really culled belongings, which was a way of getting rid of stuff we didn't love or that was simply too heavy. In hindsight we should have shed more books, but the poet and the English major couldn't part with many and the new office/library had one full wall of built-in bookshelves. Besides, the books, like the rest of our stuff except for camping gear and our clothes for the trip, were packed in a North American Van Lines transport truck that we had to neither pack nor unpack.

The night before our departure, we took in a movie at Hot Docs with the same posse of friends that had interviewed Amy when we first started dating. It was Rosie O'Donnell's *All Aboard!*, a gay-family cruise ship documentary, a perfect movie for us to contemplate on our cross-country trek. Toronto didn't loosen its grasp that easily—the pileup on Highway 400 going north delayed us for hours—but nothing could dampen the excitement we felt, beginning a new chapter in our lives. Having sold my Ford Focus wagon, we drove Amy's Volkswagen Jetta because she needed something of hers to carry forward, given the leap she especially was taking. We tent camped across the country in late April and early May. We had Quetico to ourselves and, in southwest Saskatchewan, Cypress Hills as well. These were both mythical places that had only occupied our imaginations until then but now were startlingly and beautifully real. Our only disappointment was finding Lake Louise still frozen instead of the iconic turquoise it becomes when thawed. We had given each other a knowing look as we crossed the Continental Divide, eager as we both were to start our new lives in the West.

We arrived at our new home the night before our belongings were delivered. Blissful, we slept on camping mats on the carpeted kitchen floor and awoke early with the sun streaming through the French doors. The reformed debutante was no princess with a pea. It felt as if we were floating. Around here, they say that if you are meant to stay in Nelson, things work out for you with housing and jobs. On our drive across the country, I got offered an interview for a job as a vocational rehabilitation consultant with WorkSafe-BC and I started the job within a month of arriving in Nelson, though truth be told, I was hoping to postpone the start of work until September when Amy would begin an advanced diploma in digital film at Selkirk College. As a manager at the YMCA, she went through extensive career and personality testing to ensure she was well matched to the role. In the course of that, she had validated what she knew inside, that she needed to be doing more creative work. It was more Kootenay serendipity finding out that Selkirk was starting its program in film. We hummed along, hiking on weekends, painting our new home, making it our own and hanging with friends.

We were weaving finely spun fabric together into something bigger than ourselves, incorporating silver threads of those shooting stars that remind us of the connection to the rest of the universe. The intense emotional connection leads and deepens the physical connection, one the warp and one the weft of the life we were weaving together. Fully seeing each other is the underpinning now of being able to support each other's creative endeavours.

BLESSED ARE THE NURSES

My first poetry collection, *Steeling Effects,* was an attempt not only to answer the question of how any of us, and I, in particular, end up resilient but also to leave a metaphorical road map for my children. Whatever difficult stories the twins will come to learn about their early beginnings and biological family history, they will also know they came from resilience and are themselves resilient.

Theo and Franny, or, as we called them initially, the tortoise and the hare, came to us just before they turned fifteen months, two roundish, toddling bundles. They were in shock, preverbal body shock. As I've mentioned before, for the first months, Theo lay on my tummy and chest whenever he could. He was attaching, learning to regulate with the lub-dub of my heart. He was so wise to crawl up onto me and stay there in his wordless grief. But isn't grief always, at its core, wordless? At night he cried for the only parents he'd known, his foster parents, but he laughed a lot during the day too. Franny circled, ever watchful. Cuddling attempts had to be initiated by her. We were dumbfounded that at that age, she was taking care of her brother.

One of the wisest pieces of advice I received was from a parent resource person, Liz, who advised me to put Franny on my chest, directly over my heart, when she was dysregulated. Dysregulated was code for cascading tantrums that culminated with Franny being inconsolable. It was an art form all in itself to scoop her in close at the right time so she could receive the closeness. When it worked, calm-abiding was healing for both of us; when it didn't, it caused me despair and likely her as well, a feeling that was already lodged firmly within her. A feeling I was growing accustomed to, watching these two little beings navigate adoption trauma.

The deep work of attachment is seeing each other without artifice. My wife and I did this when we were first getting to know each other. It's what everyone does who is creating a loving relationship. We found ourselves there yet again with our newly adopted children. But this time it was attachment to busy toddlers, not newborns who are built to lie skin to skin with you. "Catch them if you can" became our daily challenge. It was suggested by the adoption social workers that we take them swimming. We did this often. They have to hold on to you and learn to feel that you will be there. They learn that you will keep them safe. It mostly worked, except for the time my partner dropped our son underwater at the hot springs. The few seconds he sank below the surface felt like minutes, and then the fear and shock on his face afterwards was a mistake she still feels terrible about. He is well attached despite this one brief incident. So much of this attachment is not rational but visceral: at its very heart, love. Our predecessors, their foster parents, attached to them by being consistent and loving. That meant the twins could attach to us, despite the trauma of relocation and resettling into a brand new everything: house, parents, cribs, toys, smells and food, though we did try to make some of the dishes they were used to. Yes, we are grateful that the foster parents imprinted an attachment template through being there and loving them that first year of their lives.

After being very protective about social events and gatherings, we took Franny and Theo to Mother Goose, a nursery rhyme group, when they were approximately eighteen months old. It was in the basement of the library in a newly renovated activity room. Parents, mostly mothers, sat around in a circle and their children mostly sat in their laps while we sang songs and did dance moves facilitated by the leader. Think "The Chicken Dance" for children. What we'd been warned about by the social worker came true as we watched Franny "shop" for a mother. She would sit in everyone else's lap hoping to find it familiar. It's common among adoptive children but nevertheless it gutted us. We had to ask the circle of caregivers and parents not to let our kids sit in their laps and instead to redirect them to us. It was an uncomfortable ask with a room full of nurturers. I worried that we were being judged as control freaks. Nobody said anything out loud. We wondered whether we should be there; every time was nerve-racking. Would Franny sit with us? Would she try to sit with everyone but us? Would she see us as her primary attachment? Was she ever going to settle in to her new family and feel that we were enough?

Our twins often used to hold their little satin blankies to their faces and rub their faces together. It must have been what it felt like in their birth mother's womb, feeling each other across thin sacs in their respective darkness.

Thankfully they could reclaim this feeling without the stress hormones that must have coursed through their birth mother. They sojourned with their bio-mom and foster family but only they have accompanied each other the whole journey. I sometimes fear that we are only a sojourn for them as well but my heart and their weight every morning when they cuddle in before school tell me otherwise.

When we first adopted them, they had some mild delays in development. We took a leap of faith that their delays were a result of the adoption trauma but the truth is we didn't know. The truth is we had to be willing to love these twins as is: delays, trauma and whatever else we discovered. While this is similar with any parent, it is also different because of the question marks around genetics, pre-birth trauma and the possibility of fetal alcohol syndrome.

The bio-mom's status of prenatal alcohol consumption was not known. Where did that leave us except with subjective opinions from the pediatrician saying growth and development looked healthy, if not totally normal? He attributed this to their being twins and catch-up growth from premature birth. The social workers attributed it to interrupted attachment and early trauma. The kids lagged behind in developmental milestones until they really settled in with us. We had no idea, nor did anyone else, whether they would catch up in terms of development. We were told it was low risk. First they needed to attach to us and this is very difficult, deep work.

Our children didn't talk for a long time, until they were three years old. Nobody could definitively tell us why. Twins talking later than singles and interrupted attachment were both possibilities. Because our kids were in the foster-care system, the infant development specialist had monitored them since birth. When they moved to Nelson, their case was transferred to a very experienced and skilled specialist who came monthly to check out their development and offer us assistance to support them, such as developmental games we could play. She pointed out that our daughter was doing something advanced for her age—distracting her brother with a different toy when she wanted the toy he had. We chuckled at this move, remembering that the foster parents had told us she used to take Theo's bottle when they were babies in the same crib. And we were also reassured about our son when his fine motor skills were tested and he excelled. He could stack blocks like a five-year-old. These small signs of progress reassured us that our toddlers were not only settling in and attaching but also starting to be able to use their energy for development rather than coping with massive changes in their lives.

When the twins were eight, our son wanted to see where he was born. We arranged, through a friend in the health-care system, to go for a visit to the neonatal intensive care unit (NICU) at Kelowna General Hospital. We waited outside the locked NICU and in a few minutes were greeted by the head nurse, who led us through the wing, pointing out that they had just moved into this new space, so it wasn't actually exactly where the twins were born but it was with the same nurses and had the same equipment. The sound of monitors punctuated the air but otherwise the ward was hush and calm despite the serious issues they deal with every hour of every day with these wee babes and their families. It always strikes me in intensive care units that professionals work through daily crises yet react calmly. I guess there is no point flitting around like a stressed hummingbird; it wouldn't serve the patients or the nurses.

The nurses couldn't have been nicer touring us around. "Do you have any questions, Theo and Franny?" The twins were taking it all in quietly. "Do you want to see the incubators?"

"Okay," said Theo.

"Your incubators were a little different than these new ones. They would have looked like space helmets," the nurse said. We had pictures of them as newborns and a picture of their birth mother too. The nurses looked knowingly at the photos; their looks said, *We remember.*

One nurse, the friendliest of a friendly bunch, said, "I was adopted too. My parents came and picked me up when I was in NICU." The twins nodded. She bent down to them and said, "I remember you. You both had gorgeous dark hair when you were born. You were beautiful and we all fought over holding you."

My kids were quiet for most of that visit but afterwards they told important people in their lives that the nurses fought over them. I hope that nurse knows what a profound gift she gave them, a gift that nobody else could have given. I think she knew it when she said it, her eyes twinkling. Perhaps she longed for that same kind of story about her own start in the world. Perhaps it is I who longed to be there when they were born, time that we can never recover, though we have tried to make up for it. Our parenting occasionally takes on a feverish pace, not consciously, but nevertheless with a chorus of "We are making up for lost time, we need to love more and harder, we need to have more adventures, we need to convey we see you enough to make up for that first fifteen months when we didn't know you." That day the nurse gave them that gift and I will be forever grateful. It still makes me weep.

It was a day of gifts, it turns out. As we drove away from the hospital, I asked the kids if there was anything else they wanted to do that would help them learn about their story. My son said he wanted to meet the social worker who had helped him get adopted. We got in touch with her and though she was off work on a medical leave, recovering from a hip replacement, she was happy to meet us at a Kelowna park on that sunny day. So, there we were an hour later, visiting with the social worker who made the ultimate decision that we'd all make a good match for a family. She arrived with beach towels and candy for the kids. They were delighted but didn't want to chat too long before they ran off to climb and swing.

Here we were eight years later at a picnic table beside a playground, sitting across from the woman who saw our family forming before we did. "The kids look good. How are they doing?"

"They are pretty good. Today was a good day; I think it really impacted both of them to hear the NICU nurses say they fought over them. They get to see their foster parents later. But, yeah, trauma comes up for them. They go flight or fight on us a lot," I said.

The social worker said, "Yeah, makes sense, but good about their curiosity. Great that you keep in touch with the foster parents. I like that I facilitated the Christians and the lesbians to become friends. You look like you are doing a great job with them."

"Any suggestions for how we talk about their birth mom?" Amy asked. It was an art form knowing how and what to say to the kids depending on their developmental stage. How to say not too much, not too little, is something we fretted over many nights.

"Their birth mother had no chance of having the skills to parent the kids, but she did and does love them all. She was too ill to keep them safe." This was a welcome reassurance. We do occasionally think about the role poverty, addiction and being a visible minority play in the disproportionate number of adoptions from within these cohorts. It is uncomfortable, knowing the relative privilege we enjoy as white, educated women. It is uncomfortable knowing how privilege piles upon privilege and, likewise, hardship upon hardship.

I was and am grateful to the social worker for always being available to go the extra mile with us long after her official role of adoption social worker ended, whether it was getting in touch with the bio-mom to update her address on file so we could send letters through the third-party adoption registry or meeting us at a park while she was recovering from surgery. She is retired and she still keeps in touch. It certainly added to my already favourable view of the empaths who go into the social work profession for all the right reasons.

There are so many people along the path with my kids who held the space for them, knowing that love would get them through: the nurses, the social workers, the foster family, even the pediatrician who spent an hour on the phone with us, patiently answering our questions about their health and development, answers that would help determine our decision to adopt.

We wrote to the nurses after the NICU visit and thanked them, reminding them that they made a difference and thanking the adopted nurse in particular for giving my kids a piece of their story that is so dear to them—that they were fought over. Blessed are the nurses, the social workers and the foster parents who give over their hearts knowing they will be broken. But maybe that is a condition of love, and we all know it, more or less. We love anyway.

South Pole

My daughter is wailing again about what is not here.
Not her other mama, presently at work,
not her nana who raised her for the first year
not her blue car in the drive (see mama, above).

If she knew that olive trees don't grow here, she'd mourn them too.
Or tsetse flies, or oranges—
she's predisposed.

At a loss while she sobs, I'm reading her a book before nap,
it's called *Lost and Found*,
a boy finds a penguin,
tries to repatriate it to the South Pole,
the penguin stands forlorn on the ice
as the boy rows away in his boat.

My daughter says, "Sometimes you leave me at the South Pole and
that makes me sad."

I row through our tears,
vowing to keep her close.
Where have I left her?
Like a politician, I blame the previous administration.
The boy returns for the penguin;
eventually, they find each other and go home.

Alone, in a quiet dawn, I scan the horizon for any truth.
The gap left in the birth mother's wake is a kind of truth
but, so too, is this—
primal loss repels primal loss.
I must re-examine my own southern jaunt.
Left adrift, I, too, know despair.
We must make our way back north
to that tropic of love.

Nine Years Old

I went on a kayaking trip on Georgian Bay about twenty-five years ago, when I was living in Toronto. I was with two certified instructors who were friends. On the first evening after we set up camp, we had a kayak exit lesson at the beach. It was an exercise in not freaking out, being upside down in cold, dark water, skirted to a kayak. You had to (1) not lose your shit, (2) pull the line of the skirt to unhitch it from the cockpit's lip (coaming in boat-speak) and (3) swim deeper and away from the light to clear the boat, then emerge holding your boat.

It was good that we practised, I thought, when we got swamped by a storm that came out of nowhere across the formidable Georgian Bay. We could see it coming and though we pointed our boats to the nearest shore—a rocky beach—we knew the storm would reach us well before we hit land. The gusts came, the swells grew massive and we got churned around. Amid the terror I was feeling, there was also this: I pushed myself to exhaustion and couldn't fight anymore. I realized that the tyrant of a storm was push-ing me this way and that, up the crest of a wave and down again, sideways, backwards, but that sea kayaks are very difficult to tip if you stay relaxed. They have great secondary stability. It's humans that tip more often than not, trying to control the boat or whatever else is wreaking havoc on their perception of the world. Knowing I now had the muscle memory of how to wet-exit allowed me to surrender and it worked out. All the group made it to their own safety, strewn along a rugged shore, their kayaks still wigwagging in the wind. I cried when I got out of the boat, squatted on the rocky beach, felt the ground. This was a lesson in resilience.

Sometimes I ache when I see my preteen daughter walking around in her prepubescent innocence. I see her stick body, long and lanky, no hips to speak of, just the buds of breasts. Budding awareness too. I always thought I'd have a hard time when she was nine years old. This is the age I was sexually violated. The reality was I could barely even touch that ache when she was nine. I am relieved that, at ten, she is still in her imaginary world of dolls and drawing pretty dresses and creating Lego worlds. I see her being a kid. I know that as tough as she is on herself, she is not as tough as I was on myself. As fierce as she is on the soccer field, she is not as fierce as I was. It was life and death for me.

When I was around the age my daughter is now, I played chicken on the railway tracks with friends. The tracks were at the far edge of the farmer's field across from our house, maybe a ten-minute walk. My two friends and I stood on the tracks as a freight train approached. It was a sunny, pleasant afternoon. I don't recall the smell of fresh-cut hay so it must have been spring or summer. I recall only the smell of creosote and then the diesel from the train. I stayed the longest; the other three friends shrieked at me and the train's horn exploded at me to get off. I was frozen, compelled, as I felt the vibration of the tracks as the train neared. Then I heard the kids' voices again screaming and I stepped off just in time. A few seconds later the train ached by, going alarmingly fast even though the screech of brakes meant it had slowed. I remember the terror and the exhilaration of that. It horrified me that I had let myself get that close. I didn't want to die. I wanted to beat my friends at chicken but then I felt frozen on the tracks. I probably wanted to feel that power; the irony that I was powerless in comparison with a freight train was lost on me at that moment. Shaken as I was when I went home, I didn't tell my parents about this incident. Fortunately, though, that close call cured me of some stupidities, other than the run-of-the-mill kind: getting drunk as a teenager and driving around in boys' cars.

I couldn't identify as a victim of sexual abuse; it was just way too vulnerable. Which is why "I had sex young" became my story for a while. As if a nine-year-old could consent to such acts. It makes me sad for that young girl. Sometimes I look at my sweet daughter and grimace, seeing only vulnerability and innocence and knowing how easily it was taken from me. I have very few memories of carefree playing after nine years old. I was no longer a kid.

That year, I almost succumbed to my daughter's pleas for a phone. I would do it for safety reasons, I tell myself. It is irrational. I know she wants to text her friends, wants to imitate her moms. I know also that phones lead to anxiety for preteens. Adults can barely handle the dopamine peaks and valleys while awaiting pings and vibrations on their devices. Would a phone really help her in a jam? What kind of jam? I don't think a phone would help in the face of someone who reels children in and preys upon them, who tells them they will be harmed if they tell anyone. If I had had a phone when I was nine it wouldn't have helped one iota. I wouldn't have phoned my parents. I was across the street when I was sexually violated numerous times over months. I didn't tell them. I didn't think they would believe me. I thought I would get really messed up by my abuser too. At least that's what he told me. But most of all it was shame that kept me silent.

I want Franny to tell me if something is going on. I can barely hold the thought that she wouldn't. That is what distinguishes her from me as a kid. I hope she has no hesitation. I walked around alone for years, holding a secret whose initial act was bad enough but whose ongoing injury is even greater. If this were to happen I'm not sure I could live with myself as a parent; this is my greatest fear.

My fears for my son are different. I fear patriarchy will squash his touchy-feely self. I fear he won't be self-actualized. And while this is real, it is very different from worrying about daughters getting raped. If we consider Maslow's hierarchy of needs, with basic physiological survival needs at the bottom and self-actualization at the top of the triangle, there's a profound difference between my worries for my son and those for my daughter.

Sometimes I have all the air squeezed out of me with the thought that life is so random and much of it beyond our control. I'd like to think we have more input. But it is hard to hold that randomness of accidents, of disease. Stories, thankfully, offer a way through.

I consider how each of us deals with traumatic events beyond our control. Inconsolable looks different in a toddler than it does in a tween. It is equally devastating. Given what I know about healing from trauma, I worry that there are difficult teenage years ahead for my kids. They are dealing with trauma earlier than I did, facing things most people don't until adulthood or ever. Healing from trauma relatively early in life may have the benefit of changing one's story earlier but may feel overwhelming as a teen, when so much is about belonging and self-identity already. I wonder how Franny and I will get through her teenage years. We are so often like vinegar and oil, she and I. Fortunately, my wife is more hopeful and she is definitely more skilled than I am with youth. Her favourite age group to work with as a teacher and a camp director was middle school kids. I trust that she will relate to our kids without the heaviness that I carry. I married well.

We all fall from grace as parents. It is an impossibly difficult job to do well all the time. My parents' imperfect love will have to be enough, as my imperfect love will have to be enough for my children, and on it goes. This parenting is not for the faint of heart. It is the hardest thing. And that is where compassion for my parents starts to enter my awareness in a real way. They did their best, even if sometimes it sucked. We all have limitations. I forgive my parents for their mistakes and shortcomings. I have reckoned with this and feel at peace.

I see that my mother was constrained by the times, by her education, by moving to a brand new country where she knew nobody. I also see that I was alone. Perhaps I was supposed to be what helped her feel less alone but, although I know now that it was not my job, I also know I disappointed her.

I feel fierce about ensuring my children never feel alone, yet they will, won't they? When they see adoption through the lens of loss. The very thing I want to protect them from, I can't. When I get caught up in these kinds of thoughts, I get swallowed up by the anguish and fear that I'll be no better than my parents. Can I live with that? Can I live with being human and trying my best? Is that the question? I want to ensure my kids don't feel alone. My mother wanted to ensure she didn't feel alone. That is a significant difference. *I will see the shit out of you* seems to be my parenting motto. My ferocity comes in part from fear that I will fail as a parent. I know I can't move forward letting fear direct my parenting.

Every year we paddle down the Kootenay River from Nelson to Taghum Beach Regional Park, where the rocky banks of the river widen and offer users a respite from the current and a sandy beach at which to swim or sunbathe. This canoe trip takes only about two hours, depending upon wind and current. It is a relatively easy paddle with the current. It can be tricky because of waves at the start when the lake is still wide but narrowing into a river. We always cross to the other side of the river to look at the pictographs. Once we saw a grizzly sow and her cub ambling in a riverside meadow. On a recent paddle down the river one afternoon, our daughter was getting bored and said, "If we were in a speedboat, we'd be there by now."

"Where is *there*? We are here, just where we want to be. Paddling down the river is relaxing."

My daughter rolled her eyes as she watched the motorboats pass us by. "Boring, more like it."

I want her to be bored. I want her to take it for granted that we will always be there. If she can feel safe in a canoe going down the formidable

Kootenay River, then we've done our job. It may feel tippy but the secondary stability is sound in our canoe, as with that kayak on Georgian Bay. I want her to feel this with us so that when she is paddling her own boat through a storm, she does not give up and will trust that she can get through.

BECOMING REAL

The Velveteen Rabbit was one of my favourite childhood books. I especially loved the part about how being real is not about how you are made but is what happens to you when you are loved for a long time:

> "Does it hurt?" asked the Rabbit.
> "Sometimes," said the Skin Horse, for he was always truthful. "When you are Real you don't mind being hurt.
> … You become."

I reconnected with this book in my twenties when I was coming out. It soothed my anxious self when I worried about being shunned.

Its refrain echoed in my head again in that first year after we adopted. I have learned that becoming a *real* family is a journey. When we adopted our twins, it took about nine months to feel real. The path to feeling like a legitimate family had some obstacles, notably, the nine-month probation period during which we were not yet a legal family, and being an adoptive, transracial family parented by two moms.

Childless heterosexual couples have to explain why they don't have children. Lesbian and gay men have to explain why they want children. Perhaps that's one of the reasons why we regard it as a privilege, not a right. Amy and I were both versed in having that difficult conversation with our parents, from the days of coming out. We both had to be real because we had no choice. Coming out is a good training ground for any other necessary conversations with parents about adopting children.

I remember making dinner for my partner's parents so we could talk to them about starting a family. "Mom, Dad, Jane and I want to have a family. We've started the adoption process," Amy said. There was silence at the table; I stared into my salad and examined the shredded beets.

Finally, after he'd gathered his wits and remembered to be polite, my father-in-law said, "Congratulations. Wow, that is a big deal." Amy's mother remained silent. Later, I held my partner as she wept, knowing that when her brother had announced he and his wife were expecting their first child, my mother-in-law had said it was the happiest day of her life.

That silence smashed up against our expectations that they would be happy for us. In other times I may have been bitter about that silence, assuming it meant this or that, all bad. These days, I try to hold space for other possibilities, for writing, if nothing else, is an act of empathy. Perhaps my mother-in-law was worrying about us having to navigate homophobia with children or worrying about us getting our hearts broken by broken children. Maybe.

Empathy is sort of like triple-glazed windows: it costs a lot at the beginning but the payoff is over the long term. How the cost of judgment is like the cost of not replacing those old windows; you end up never sitting by the window looking out at the lake because of the draft, and there is always a sense of unease like that of burning dollar bills in the furnace, the unease of knowing the uninhabitable cold is curling its frozen fingers through the cracks and tapping on your shoulder. Then, before you know it, you've retreated to your bed under a blanket instead of looking out the window at the lake and mountains.

There were many external as well as internal reasons we didn't feel like "real parents." That first phone call with the Ministry of Children and Family Development to start the information-gathering process, when the intake social worker asked my name and then my husband's name, assuming we were a heterosexual couple, was first among them. Throughout the adoption process, we were told consistently that it would probably take longer to find a match for us because we were not the "ideal" family. The notion that a family is a mom, a dad and children, and that anything else is somehow less, is still a deeply held belief. The foster parents initially opposed the match, so we were subjected to additional screening and scrutiny. This was another step on the journey to becoming real.

I have witnessed a range of reactions to our twins having two moms, from blank expressions to questions about whether they'll have any male role models. Occasionally, when I still feel insecure about being a mother or need to feel legitimized, I turn to science. All the studies say that children of gay and lesbian parents do as well as children of heterosexual parents in terms of emotional, cognitive, social and sexuality functioning. Some studies suggest that children of lesbian parents do better than those of heterosexuals in terms of being more confident and less aggressive. In other words, it is the quality of the relationships, not the gender of the parents, that matters. The only negative indicator that differentiates children of same-sex parents from children of heterosexual parents is the social stigma they may face because of their parents' sexual orientation.

We are no strangers to discrimination, so my partner and I feel well equipped to give our children the tools they need to face discrimination while keeping their selves intact. I didn't realize until I had kids that the years I spent feeling painfully ashamed of my sexuality and the journey to learning to take my space and place in the world were merely a training ground for what was to come later. Of course, having two moms has not been and will not be the only cause of discrimination our children face. Our children do not look like us. Although my partner is half West Asian, we both "look" Caucasian, while the twins are biracial: South Asian and likely Caucasian. This leads to people asking us where the children are from or whose they are. This simply would not be asked if they didn't have brown skin.

We've had flight attendants speaking Spanish to our kids. When one asked where they were from, I answered "Canada." I could tell from her bewildered look that she had the best of intentions. I chose to educate her so she might hold her racism in check next time. "Their birth mom is South Asian. They are Canadian. Canadians come in all colours."

"Oh, I could have sworn they were Central American," she replied.

Our kids will probably question their identities at some point, or many points, along the way. We thought about this and were initially wary of unduly burdening them. But after copious reading about this issue, fretting over what our children would have to deal with because they look different from us and most other people in our small town, we ultimately came to the conclusion that loving the children, exposing them to their cultural heritages and to other transracial adoptees would be enough to usher them through to adulthood with a healthy sense of self. We committed to taking them to places where they would see many people who look like them, such as our old neighbourhood in Toronto, or South Asia. Thankfully, on this matter, we also had good support from our social workers, who reminded us of our strengths as a family and believed in us.

For many months after we brought them home, I referred to my children simply by their names, avoiding any familial references. The first time I uttered "my son and daughter," I took a deep breath first, unable to look the other person in the eye and ready to bolt should my declaration be challenged. It was the same feeling I had during my long process of coming out, taking those first, tentative steps to say my partner's name to a stranger. I was expert at using gender-neutral pronouns when describing my personal life and could censor myself with ease. I didn't feel like my relationship was legitimate when coming out, just as I didn't feel legitimate as a parent at first.

This experience of becoming a "real" family has taught me many things so far, perhaps most importantly that most people are open and curious. Even if a handful are being judgmental, most are open to changing their judgments, especially when faced with a two-year-old child's toothy grin. In that instant, there is an opportunity to connect and break down barriers, just as we discovered while living with our children's foster family.

It took me a long time to believe I was worthy of having a family. I was happy to be a mother of young children in my forties. I know myself well and know what I have to give to kids. The process of starting a family was so much more grounded and positive than the process of coming out, twenty years before. Devoid of role models, split in two, my very private lesbian life and the rest of me, I had a fear of being caught by roommates during private displays of affection, for there were no public displays of affection then. With each telling, I wondered if I'd be completely rejected and lose someone in my life. It was an emotional roller coaster. I didn't realize then that I was becoming more resilient to deal with future challenges. I see many adoptive parents treading in the unfamiliar territory of being excluded because of their differences. As lesbians, we are well equipped to give our children tools to meet these challenges head-on, as versed as we are in singing a different tune most of our lives.

These days, when we visit the foster parents, we are given a room with a double bed, which would have been unimaginable after our initial meeting. Once they even babysat our twins and let us stay in their honeymoon suite, which they normally rent out for romantic getaways. We happily took them up on this offer, all the while laughing at the irony and marvelling at how far we'd all come. They told us they thought we were the best parents for our kids and said we were doing a great job and that it was challenging their world view that kids need a mom and a dad to be well adjusted. Heck, if a lesbian couple can spend every waking moment for two weeks with a

Christian fundamentalist couple and come out at the end as friends, there is hope in the world.

About a year after our adoption order was granted, we were on another flight to Florida. We had many stopovers and multiple seatmates on the trip and were asked many times where our children were from and whose children they were. In answering one of the dozens of questions, I caught myself saying "my son and daughter …" It just rolled off my tongue. There I was, sitting in my aisle seat, my children beside me, with a glimmer in my eye. My partner didn't even notice, because there was nothing strange in this sentence anymore. She was feeling real as well. She, too, has a son and daughter now.

On this trip, we saw my in-laws, who were so taken by their new grandchildren that they sent boxes of gifts every few weeks and swelled with pride when telling friends or strangers about their newest family members. Seeing two happy parents with two happy, engaged, laughing, tumbling children had melted away their concerns. All five of the cousins, Amy's brother's three kids and our two, descend on St. Louis for the annual "G Camp." Amy accompanies them, though—they just aren't ready to be away from us for that long. On those trips, Theo proudly wears his Dodgers baseball cap to irk his grandparents, who are staunch Cardinals fans. Franny and her grandmother go off shopping for the latest fashions. I have a needlepointed personalized Christmas stocking from my mother-in-law. We are happily surprised by the turnaround and acceptance we feel from Amy's parents.

One evening, as I was lying beside Franny while she went to sleep, she started touching my arm and saying "Mom" over and over while looking into my eyes.

"Mom, Mom." It was like she was getting it and reflecting to me that it was indeed real.

I returned her big gaze and said, "Yes, I am your mom."

We *become*.

WHY DO YOU
HAVE TO BE SO JOYFUL?

"Why do you have to be so joyful?" Franny asks as she trudges through old-growth cedars to spread the ashes of our beloved golden retriever, Darwin. We had chosen to hike up Old Glory Mountain on a crisp October day, a hike Darwin had done with us a few times when alive, a hike that became a symbol of the macho persona we had constructed for him. In his final days, he was Old Glory, holding court under a shade tree, teaching us how to love and let go. I laugh at her question and am delighted. I don't think I could have been accused of joyfulness at many points in my life. Brooding, self-critical, harsh, yes, but joyful? Rather, I think there are episodes of joy but they are punctuated by struggle and doubt as I try to align my story with new information. She is challenging my story about myself.

I used to think happiness was for stupid people, people who were incapable of deconstructing and analysis. I spent a long time deconstructing, for which I'm grateful. It leads to a kind of happiness that is bittersweet, not the ease of unconsciousness but the worthy labour that leads to an examined life. Ever since I read Jack Gilbert's "A Brief for the Defense," I have been drawn to his words:

> We must risk delight. We can do without pleasure,
> but not delight. Not enjoyment. We must have
> the stubbornness to accept our gladness in the ruthless
> furnace of this world.

I have been conscious of helping my son and daughter develop joy and gratitude pathways in their brains. Nothing like having children to force one to look in the mirror. It is my hope that my daughter's already grooved pavement toward disappointment is smoothed out by being well loved. Frequently, Franny experiences things as *not enough*. Theo is frequently very hard on himself and easily slips into *I am no good* instead of *I don't know how to do this*. I suspect these propensities have deep roots in adoption trauma but it doesn't really matter where it came from. It is our job to be our own amateur cartographers and to help our children develop new road maps.

My son loves the song "I'm Still Standing" by Elton John. It was featured in the movie *Sing* when the character Johnny HD was missing his father. I don't know if the bit about the father is coincidental but it is interesting. This makes me hopeful. Theo is still standing, after a tough start to his life. He's running and jumping too. It is not a popular song among his peers and it is quite a departure from AC/DC and hip hop, which he normally listens to, but he loves that song. I make meaning out of this but I don't know if it's his meaning.

In my states of suffering over the years, I walked miles to look for truth. I had doubts about coming out, about having children, and I still have doubts about parenting decisions. Each time I've examined doubt, fear drives it and when I work through fear, I settle in to decisions and ways of being that feel right. And then my story changes to incorporate new truths. Until recently, I didn't fully embrace the fact that our truth changes with every step. By the time you read this, your truth will change too. I never expected to be happily married. When I was coming out, I doubted that ordinary joys like marriage and children were possible. So I flipped the bird to all of it in my twenties. I was sad when I was coming out. I didn't think I'd be allowed to love without a shroud of secrecy, didn't think we would achieve the right to marry. The thought of having children was tinged with all the sadness of all the lesbians I'd ever known who'd lost custody or had to be in the closet until their kids grew up so they would not be taken away. It's a particular joy accessible to those who never assumed they would have access.

As the writer Andrew Solomon said, "I didn't expect those ordinary joys to be available to me. The seeds of joy were in those early sadnesses. Hence ordinary joy is still extraordinary to me." Even fighting with a partner was a privilege I didn't have in the early days: two friends wouldn't fight like that. We couldn't in our apartment, with our landlords living below us; we couldn't when we lived with roommates either. Sex was a sordid affair, though we were probably fooling no one.

I never thought a source of my resilience would be wrestling my humanity from those who would try to take it. I haven't quite evolved enough to thank my brother for his behaviour that Christmas many years ago but I do know that how I've lived with that and responded to it is part of what's made me who I am. I couldn't have written the poems I have without being fuelled by that and other injustices. We hopefully get to a place of gratitude and acceptance for all of who we are.

I spent a long time forging meaning. It took me a while to get to changing the world. How do I change the world? I came out. I walk through airports with my wife and our children and we don't hide being a family. The personal really is the political after all. I wrote a long ode to the queer community, a book called *Acquired Community*.

I remember eating the best ice cream of my life at Kawartha Dairy in Ontario. I ordered the peach flavour. I was in a bliss of cold peach on a hot summer's day. I was with my partner at the time, having driven in for a treat from a cabin we were renting. The peach ice cream was so good, we returned the next day, knowing the lineup would be just as long. I felt a churning in my stomach on the way there and decided I wouldn't get my hopes up about the peach; in fact I decided not to even order the peach because what if it wasn't as good? What if they had none left? It was vulnerable, too vulnerable to feel that much joy and have it taken away, so I wouldn't put myself in that position. I grappled back and forth internally. *Order the peach. No, don't. Order raspberry ripple, it'll be good too.* We arrived and stood in line. I looked at their large board that lists the flavours of the day. No peach. *See*, my brain said, *everything you love is precarious. See, you were right to protect against that fresh-peach-ice-cream joy.* I have reflected on this experience and I know that now I would go back wholeheartedly wanting and planning to order the peach, no holding back. I would be willing to face the disappointment of really wanting and not getting the peach.

Recently, on vacation, my kids were playing on a huge, inflatable, green and yellow play structure in Osoyoos Lake. It was like a ninja warrior obstacle course on water. I looked out from the beach to check on them. I recognized my son by his knobby, brown knees from thirty metres away. A second later he waved at me. My heart skipped a beat, my eyes wet behind my Ray-Bans. His knees, his wave from thirty metres away, is all it took. It feels like some sort of rich and unbidden gift to feel this love.

I have two amazing children. I am in love and loved. We live where we choose. I enjoy my work, both as an ergonomist and as a writer. My life is not in danger; I have seen laws and attitudes change in my lifetime toward more equality. I have enough money, love and even beauty. I experience many points of joy unbidden. I sometimes wonder if it will all evaporate, but that is just catastrophizing joy, as Brené Brown so eloquently puts it. "How many of you have stood over your child while they are sleeping and thought 'Oh my God, I love you, like, so much I can't breathe,' and in that split second pictured something horrific happening to your child. ... This is the concept of foreboding joy." She says when we lose our tolerance for vulnerability, joy becomes foreboding. The doubt gives the illusion of protection. It is small courage indeed to lean into that feeling. My capacity for joy is a work in progress, as is my capacity for vulnerability. My children bring out the best of me in this regard. I know there is nothing better than a day spent with my wife and kids when we all hang out together, present with each other. I know that to be alive is to experience pain. I no longer need to prove it to those around me. I now know it is to experience joy as well. Mostly I try to be thankful I can feel and, as a result, I can live my best life. I also work out, strengthening my body for the times I will inevitably need more strength. Heartbreak in a heart-opened life is guaranteed but I'd rather love and be loved and live with the heartache of loss, thanks.

None of us know how the story ends so we may as well be grateful for and delight in the journey. I'm revising my story to include being joyful. It's a good antidote to shame. My daughter will have to live with it, this joy that flourishes from the tangled undergrowth of my life.

Early-Morning Clarity

Most mornings I gingerly step down the creaky stairs of our Victorian house at least an hour before the rest of my family for my quiet mug of tea and a few pages of writing. On my way to the kettle, I look out of the living room window, north, across Kootenay Lake at Elephant Mountain, aptly named both for its features and for its bulk. Even in the early-morning darkness it is seldom dark enough to make the mountain invisible. In winter the mountain is illuminated by snow; in summer dusk creeps into the sky by 4:00 a.m. The mountain, like most in the Selkirk range, is heavily treed, so all year round we get conifer green, and in early May, the chartreuse of aspen buds. The fall is a gold blaze of aspen and larch.

This backdrop to our town also serves as a weather gauge. I marvel at the vertical element to weather, one that I was unaware of growing up in largely horizontal eastern Ontario. The snow descends down the mountain in November and stays for months, then ascends daily in April until it disappears. When snow covers the top of the mountain ridge, it is said, the bears go into hibernation. In spring, local wisdom says, one must not plant a garden until the snow has melted from its long, flat back. The outline of the elephant is there: its trunk faces west and its enormous eye is in fact the rocky promontory and pinnacle of the very popular Pulpit hike. So iconic is this Nelson hike, highlighting the fit lifestyle, that I intentionally hiked it after my very first day of work in Nelson, badly spraining my ankle on the perilous, dusty descent. Amy supported me down as I hobbled and scuttled on my butt. That descent is now much less perilous since more switchbacks and steps have mellowed grades where there were once steep slopes of eroding soil that turned to dust by midsummer. Some locals think taming the trail is acquiescence to a too-often manicured world but the sheer number of boots on ground dictates erosion control and more safety. I hobbled around for the first couple of weeks of my orientation and training at WorkSafeBC after my determination to have work-life balance. A better foreshadowing I could not have made up.

It is hard to see the entirety of the mountain because it is so big and close, though if you get up a little higher than we live in town, the flagpole with the tattered, weather-beaten Canadian flag is visible. The flagpole hike is also a popular hike for locals, though twice the length and more than twice the elevation of Pulpit. The view is lovely but not spectacular, compared with some of the larger peaks around.

I feel disoriented when the low clouds sit in our narrow valley for days in winter, totally obscuring Elephant Mountain and all the other shoulders of mountains that surround our town. I don't like the days that stretch into weeks of being socked in with low cloud but not for the same reason that most others don't like it. It doesn't look like I'm in the mountains at all. It is familiar and I feel comfort with mock flatness, as opposed to the passion I feel when I'm in the mountains, a constant reminder that I'm small. Perhaps I need to have my ego wiped out by landscape.

People go to the ski hill on cloudy days just to get above the clouds even if they aren't skiers. We often go up and snowshoe among the trees, up steep grades and back down. We often end up at the ski lodge. To go to the lodge and gaze at the clear blue sky and the dazzling white peaks is to seek clarity and sunshine in communion with all the other skiers and non-skiers alike. It takes me back to my blue wonder as a child looking out at that endless sky from the cockpit.

On one particular morning, when Amy and I were driving to an appointment rather than to go outdoor adventuring, we were late. It's easy in this smallish town to be on "Kootenay time," a euphemism for being late, usually due to hanging about, running into a friend or doing nothing. This was New York City time, lateness due to trying to accomplish too much, in my case, one more email plus a shower before driving to a meeting with Franny's art therapist for an end-of-session check-in.

Amy was pissed off as I walked up our stone steps to the car. I'd made her anxious and frustrated that we would be inconveniencing Laura, the art therapist, with whom we entrusted our daughter's emotional health and therapeutic growth. "Why are you late? Why can't you just be on time? You know how I hate being late, how I hate stressing about getting there," she unleashed as I got in the car.

It was a frigid morning, as cold as it gets here. The windshield already scraped by waiting Amy, we set off in that frozen compartment, with one minute to do a five-minute drive. The cold, when it plummeted to anything below minus ten degrees Celsius, occasionally made our car's electronic things malfunction until they warmed. Our radio, with the volume stuck on loud on an '80s satellite station, blared "Keep On Loving You" by REO Speedwagon.

Our argument escalated until it crescendoed with the chorus and we looked at each other realizing the absurdity. The damn radio would not be ignored. *I'm gonna keep on loving you, cause it's the only thing I wanna do. I don't wanna sleep, I just wanna keep on lovin' you.* We both broke out into a fit of laughter. A radio intervention conspired to make us stop and see what mattered, helped us let go of a minor infraction. As we started the meeting, we had a good laugh about it with Laura.

We have spirited disagreements and raise our voices. Sometimes there are tears. Most often, though, there is love and a lot of it. Amy and I have managed to support each other through the sometimes rocky journey of parenthood, and most often we've been able to laugh at the end of even the tough days.

On Fridays at lunch, we stop whatever other important things we are doing, usually making movies or writing books, and ski or hike up Pulpit and have lunch. It brings us back to each other. We don't allow the whole conversation to be about our children, though sometimes a good chunk is. We share what's going on in our heads, our creative thoughts, our fears. We find our way back to one another, for a lot can happen in a week, it seems. We need these frequent reminders that we enjoy hanging out together. The mundane logistics of ferrying kids to sports, music, art and appointments threaten to sink us sometimes. It's a logistics-free lunch, which we mostly abide.

Having two moms hover is often redundant with the morning routine. The kids make their own lunches and can pretty much take care of themselves in the morning. Theo still reaches his arms around one of us for cuddle time every morning and reaches those same arms out to wrestle his sister, which she counters with words that jar and sting. Mostly, though, mornings are easier than at any other time since we brought them home, periodic preteen hormone surges notwithstanding. Maybe I am naive but I have no doubt that we will abide by REO Speedwagon's words.

Elephant Mountain looms outside our front window. I used to think the elephant in the room was trauma; now I think it's joy. Both are equally precarious, yet the big chunk of granite facing me every morning brings me back to that hard-won joy. That rocky precipice sticking out of the mountain, from which we look down for our house: the green metal roof, the yellow siding. It seems tiny from the lookout, yet it contains all of our memories of being a family. We see the grid of our town, interrupted by granite, surrounded by mountains and trees in every direction. We are in the middle of it all. The mighty Kootenay River takes all our joy, our sorrow, even our trauma, and deposits some of it along its banks, or along the banks of the Columbia River into which it flows. Perhaps it washes the rest out to sea.

NOTES

The poems "Out of the Blue" (p. 20), "Tolerance" (p. 37), "Born Again" (p. 102), and "Come Out" (p. 109) were previously published in *Acquired Community* (Caitlin Press, 2016). The poems "Teenagers Talk About Sex" (p. 31), "Sweetness" (p. 51), "Intensive Care" (p. 64), "Skunk Cabbage" (p. 129), "Fever of Gratitude" (p. 152), and "South Pole" (p. 170) were previously published in *Steeling Effects* (Caitlin Press, 2014). The poem on page 99 was excerpted from *It Hurt, That's All I Know* (Nose in Book Press, 2017).

Early versions of some of the text appears in the following anthologies:
"What If Your Kids Grow Up To Be Straight?" *Swelling With Pride: Queer Conception and Adoption Stories*, ed. Sara Graefe (Caitlin Press, 2018).
"Conceiving Family" *Out Proud: Stories of Pride, Courage and Social Justice*, ed. Douglas Gosse (Breakwater Books, 2014).
"Becoming Real" *Somebody's Child: Essays on Adoption*, eds. Bruce Gillespie & Lynne Van Luven (Touchwood Editions, 2011).

Other references:
p. 110, "Coping" by Audre Lorde, *The Black Unicorn: Poems* (W.W. Norton, 1978).
p. 112, *The Primal Wound: Understanding the Adopted Child*, by Nancy Newton Verrier (Gateway Press, 1993).
p. 136, Rabbi Danya Ruttenberg on Judaism and forgiveness (*Tapestry*, October 25, 2018, CBC Radio).
p. 150, Anne Enright on writing as shame management (*The Enright Files*, June 2018, CBC Ideas).
p. 159, "In Blackwater Woods" by Mary Oliver, *American Primitive* (Back Bay Books, 1983).
p. 182, "A Brief for the Defense" by Jack Gilbert, *Refusing Heaven: Poems* (Alfred A. Knopf, 2005).
p. 183, "How the Worst Moments in Our Lives Make Us Who We Are," Andrew Solomon, TED2014.
p. 185, "Daring Classrooms," Brené Brown, SXSW EDU Conference, 2017.

ACKNOWLEDGEMENTS

To my wife, Amy Bohigian, whose encouragement and generous reading of many drafts have made this memoir possible.

To my Roombas writing group: Linda, Bobbie and Susan, and my B&I writing group: Anne, Rita, Verna, Sarah, Jenny and Vangie, all who have read many drafts.

To Sara Graefe for her patient and thorough editing and ushering of a poet through her first prose manuscript.

To my brother Justin, who supported and encouraged me along the way.

To my mother, Patricia Byers, for her support.

To Eimnear Laffan, whose musings about doubt's meaning in Gaelic led me to a book title.

To Susan Andrews Grace for her artistic query into doubt and her course "Writing With Doubt."

To Deryn Collier for talking me down from a deep dive into doubt.

To Marilyn Lee for her generous reading.

To many friends who have patiently listened and offered support and suggestions as I told some of these stories around the campfire.

To my publisher, Vici Johnstone, whose integrity shines. Thank you for championing voices that may not otherwise be heard. And to her wonderful team at Caitlin Press.

ABOUT THE AUTHOR

JANE BYERS has published two poetry collections, *Acquired Community* (Caitlin Press, 2016), a 2017 Goldie Award Winner for Poetry and *Steeling Effects* (Caitlin Press, 2014), and a chapbook, *It Hurt, That's All I Know* (Nose in Book Publishing, 2017). She has co-written two award-winning documentary films, *Only in Nelson* and *Conceiving Family*. She was the 2018 Writer-in-Residence for Simon Fraser University's ALOT Archives. She has had poems and essays published in anthologies and literary journals in Canada, the US and England, including Best Canadian Poetry 2014.

Her tween twins are embarrassed by everything parental, including the fact that they have one mother who is a writer and one who is a filmmaker. Being introduced after being cajoled and occasionally dragged to book launches and movie premieres from their home in the Southern Interior of British Columbia further mortifies them.

You can connect with Jane at janebyerspoetry.com and on her blog: janecookswhitewater.wordpress.com.